AN EYE FOR THE STAGE

AN EYE FOR THE STAGE

The Tobin Collection of Theatre Arts at the McNay Art Museum

Jody Blake

WITH A FOREWORD AND ESSAY BY

William J. Chiego

The McNay

THE MARION KOOGLER McNAY ART MUSEUM

San Antonio, Texas

This publication is made possible by the generous underwriting of the Tobin Endowment.

Copyright © 2004 by The Marion Koogler McNay Art Museum

All rights reserved. No part of this publication may be reproduced, stored in a retrieval system, or transmitted in any form or by any means, electronic, mechanical, photocopying, or otherwise, without prior written permission from the publisher, except by a reviewer who wishes to quote brief passages in connection with a review written for inclusion in a magazine, newspaper, or broadcast.

The Marion Koogler McNay Art Museum
6000 North New Braunfels
P. O. Box 6069
San Antonio, Texas 78209-0069
www.McNayArt.org

An Eye for the Stage is available for purchase through the McNay Art Museum Store
6000 North New Braunfels
P. O. Box 6069
San Antonio, Texas 78209-0069
210.805.1732

Library of Congress Control Number: 2004100305
ISBN: 0-916677-50-8

Endsheets: Paul Knauerhase, Scene design for Temple of Isis in *Die Zauberflöte (The Magic Flute)*, 1904 (detail), see plate 10
Page 2: Illustration of a Roman theatre from Terence, *Comoediae*, woodcut with hand coloring, image 9⅝ × 6⅝ in. Strasbourg: Johann Reinhard Grüninger, 1496. Gift of Robert L. B. Tobin, TL1984.1.659
Page 3: Alexandre Manceau, French, 1817–1865, after Maurice Sand, French, 1823–1889. Illustration of Pantalone from Maurice Sand, *Masques et Bouffons (Comédie Italienne)*, Vol. 2, etching with hand coloring, page 10½ × 7 in. Paris: Michel Lévy Frères, 1860. Gift of Robert L. B. Tobin, TL1984.1.48
Page 5: Jean Eckart and William Eckart, Scene design for Open a New Window, Act I, Scene 5 in *Mame*, 1966 (detail), see plate 54
Page 6: Tobin Library and Gallery at the McNay
Page 8: McNay Art Museum

Edited by Michelle Piranio
Proofread by Sharon Vonasch
Typeset by Jennifer Sugden
Designed by Jeff Wincapaw
Color separations by iocolor, Seattle
Produced by Marquand Books, Inc., Seattle
 www.marquand.com
Printed and bound by C&C Offset Printing Co., Ltd., China

Photography credits:
Historical and family photographs courtesy of the Estate of Robert L. B. Tobin, pp. 10, 42, 52, 68, 76–81; the McNay Art Museum Archives, pp. 15, 82, 85, and 87; and the collection of Linda M. Hardberger, p. 95
Photographs of the McNay Art Museum and Tobin Library and Gallery, pp. 8–9 by Hester + Hardaway
Photograph of the Tobin Library staircase, p. 87, by James McNeel Keller
All art objects were photographed by Michael Jay Smith.

Copyright credits:
Images of the McNay Art Museum and Tobin Library and Gallery, pp. 8–9 © 1997 Hester + Hardaway
Photograph of the Tobin Library staircase, p. 87 © 1984 James McNeel Keller
Robert L. B. Tobin, p. 76 © Karsh, Ottawa
Benois: © 2004 Artists Rights Society (ARS), New York/ADAGP, Paris
Cocteau: © 2004 Artists Rights Society (ARS), New York/ADAGP, Paris
de Chirico:© 2004 Artists Rights Society (ARS), New York/SIAE, Rome
Fini: © 2004 Artists Rights Society (ARS), New York/ADAGP, Paris
Gontcharova: © 2004 Artists Rights Society (ARS), New York/ADAGP, Paris
Indiana: © 2004 Morgan Art Foundation, Ltd./Artists Rights Society (ARS), New York
Larionov: © 2004 Artists Rights Society (ARS), New York/ADAGP, Paris
Léger: © 2004 Artists Rights Society (ARS), New York/ADAGP, Paris
Matisse: © 2004 Succession H. Matisse, Paris/Artists Rights Society (ARS), New York
Picasso: © 2004 Estate of Pablo Picasso, Artists Rights Society (ARS), New York
Smith: Courtesy of Rosaria Sinisi, Brooklyn, New York
Wilson: Courtesy Byrd Hoffman Water Mill Foundation

PREFACE   6
J. Bruce Bugg Jr.

FOREWORD   7
William J. Chiego

THE TOBIN COLLECTION
OF THEATRE ARTS AT
THE MCNAY ART MUSEUM   11
Jody Blake

CONTENTS

15   RARE BOOKS AND PAST PERFORMANCES

20   OPERAS CLASSIC AND CONTEMPORARY

26   SHAKESPEAREAN STAGES FROM BRITAIN TO AMERICA

32   EDWARD GORDON CRAIG'S NEW STAGECRAFT

36   OUT OF RUSSIA

42   NATALIA GONTCHAROVA: FOLKLORE AND FINE ART

46   FROM STUDIOS TO STAGES IN MODERNIST PARIS

52   EUGENE BERMAN, NEO-ROMANTIC

56   THE GOLDEN AGE OF THE BROADWAY MUSICAL

62   BALLETS AND OPERAS OF AMERICAN LIFE

68   ROBERT INDIANA: THE MOTHER OF US ALL

72   THE MAQUETTE AND CONTEMPORARY THEATRE

ROBERT L.B. TOBIN
AND THE THEATRE   77
Jody Blake

ROBERT L.B. TOBIN
AND THE MCNAY   83
William J. Chiego

TRIBUTES TO
ROBERT L.B. TOBIN   91

A PERSONAL REMEMBRANCE   94
Linda Hardberger

TOBIN COLLECTION
PUBLICATIONS   96

PREFACE

In private conversations with Robert L. B. Tobin, we always referred to the objects in his cherished collection of theatre designs and books as his "children" and to the Tobin Wing at the McNay Art Museum as the house that his mother, Margaret Lynn Batts Tobin, built for them. We embraced the analogy, and so it was, is, and always will be that the Tobin Wing very much represents Robert's gift to humanity —a gift of himself, his keen eye and skill, and his interest in and appreciation for the world of theatre arts.

On this, the seventieth anniversary of the birth of Robert L. B. Tobin, and the twentieth anniversary of the opening of the Tobin Wing at the McNay, Leroy G. Denman Jr. and I, as co-trustees of the Tobin Endowment, celebrate the publication of this book as a fitting tribute to the life of this remarkable man.

J. Bruce Bugg Jr.
Co-Trustee, Tobin Endowment

FOREWORD

An Eye for the Stage marks the twentieth anniversary of the Tobin Wing of the McNay Art Museum, the home of the Tobin Collection of Theatre Arts. This volume pays homage to Robert L. B. Tobin and his remarkable collection of theatre arts, and is intended to provide for the nonspecialist a window into this vast and varied collection. The most comprehensive overview to date, it reproduces key works from each important area of the collection and includes a history of the collection and of Tobin's long association with this museum.

As we celebrate this important milestone, the McNay is poised to receive the final gift of the Tobin Collection of Theatre Arts planned by Mr. Tobin before his death. The gathering of this great collection under one roof reinforces the reputation of the McNay as a national center for the study and appreciation of the theatre arts, making us unique among American art museums. It also signals a renewal of our efforts to make this collection accessible to as many people as possible, to see it actively used by students of all ages.

With the opening of the Tobin Wing in 1984 there began a parade of enlightening exhibitions that presented the riches of the collection to our public and, through many publications, to the wider world. These exhibitions were the result of a fruitful collaboration between Robert Tobin and Linda Hardberger, curator of the Tobin Collection of Theatre Arts from 1984 until her retirement from the post in 2001.

I am grateful to Jody Blake, curator of the Tobin Collection of Theatre Arts since 2002, for her dedicated work in producing this book for the anniversary of the Tobin Wing. Her fine selections and excellent commentary will open up the collection to a much broader audience. I would also like to thank public and media relations manager Margaret Anne Lara, collections manager Heather Lammers, curatorial assistant Lisa Endresen, Tobin intern Catherine Walworth, librarians Ann Jones and David Hughes, and library assistant Heather Ferguson.

I gratefully acknowledge the Tobin Endowment and its co-trustees J. Bruce Bugg Jr. and Leroy G. Denman Jr. for generously underwriting this publication; providing ongoing support for the operation of the Tobin Wing, including internships in theatre arts; and making available special funds to help celebrate this anniversary. I would also like to thank the Tobin Foundation for Theatre Arts, its president Mel Weingart, and his fellow directors Linda Hardberger and Robert Perdziola for making possible a program of exhibitions at the McNay. In addition, we appreciate their continuing acquisitions to augment the Tobin Collection. Because of the generosity of the Tobin Endowment and the Tobin Foundation we are able to fulfill Robert Tobin's dream of a living and growing collection.

William J. Chiego
Director

McNay Art Museum Board of Trustees

TRUSTEES

Mr. Thomas C. Frost
Chairman
Mrs. Arthur T. Stieren
President
Mrs. L. Lowry Mays
Vice President
Mrs. Ben F. Foster Jr.
Secretary
Mr. Allan G. Paterson Jr.
Treasurer

Mrs. Michael Baucum
Mrs. William J. Block
Mr. J. Bruce Bugg Jr.
Mr. Jonathan C. Calvert
Francisco G. Cigarroa, M.D.
Mr. E. H. Corrigan
Mrs. Howard Halff
Mrs. Hugh Halff Jr.
Mrs. J. R. Hurd
Ms. Karen Jennings
Mr. Walter Nold Mathis
Mr. William H. McCartney
Mr. Jesse H. Oppenheimer
Mr. W. Lawrence Walker Jr.
Mr. Joe M. Westheimer Jr.

HONORARY TRUSTEES

Mr. Robert Halff
Mrs. Nancy B. Hamon
Mrs. Nancy B. Negley

EMERITUS TRUSTEES

Mr. Walter F. Brown
Mrs. George J. Condos
Mr. Alan W. Dreeben
Mr. George H. Ensley
Mr. Charles E. Foster
Mr. George C. Hixon
Mrs. H. T. Johnson
Jeanne Lang Mathews
Mrs. B. J. McCombs
Mr. Michael J. C. Roth
Ethel Thomson Runion
Mr. Thomas R. Semmes
Alice C. Simkins
Mr. Gaines Voigt
Mr. Harold J. Wood

ADVISORY TRUSTEES

Mr. Harry F. Schwethelm Jr.
President, Friends of the McNay
Mrs. Gerald Beverly
Docent Chairman

Jody Blake

THE TOBIN COLLECTION OF THEATRE ARTS AT THE MCNAY ART MUSEUM

The Tobin Collection of Theatre Arts, like the McNay Art Museum itself, has the reputation of being a rare gem respected for its distinctive personality and exemplary quality. Both the McNay and the Tobin Collection reflect the discerning tastes of individual collectors with an extraordinary "eye" for art, namely, Marion Koogler McNay and Robert L. B. Tobin, respectively.

Tobin's collection grew out of his great passion for theatre. Scene and costume designs are invaluable documents of live performances, which are themselves ephemeral. They record stage designers' intentions and, long after the performance is over, continue to evoke the theatrical experience. Theatre designs, however, can also be appreciated as works of visual art in their own right, as an integral part of the history of American and European art.

The Tobin Collection, which includes more than 10,000 objects, is already extraordinary in its scope and quality. In 2004, marking the twentieth anniversary of the Tobin Wing, the McNay will receive the next major gift of theatre designs from Tobin's collection. Designs from the sixteenth to nineteenth centuries, by artists from Jacques Callot to Victor St. Léon, will provide valuable historical background for the twentieth-century American and European theatre designs presented to the McNay between 1999 and 2002.

Particular strengths of the Tobin Collection include: Renaissance and Baroque designs and rare books; designs for theatre classics, in particular Shakespeare plays; designs for opera, including the contemporary repertoire; designs for Broadway musicals; and designs by those whom Tobin called "artists in the theatre," including the painters of the Ballets Russes. Also notable are the number of designers and artists whose work is represented in great depth, among them Edward Gordon Craig, Natalia Gontcharova, Eugene Berman, and Robert Indiana.

Robert L. B. Tobin at the exhibition of his collection at the Grolier Club, New York City, 1983.

Jacques Callot
French, 1592–1635
after designs by Giulio Parigi, Italian, 1580–1635

Scene design for The Burning of Aleppo, Act V (finale) in *Il Solimano,* 1620
Etching, plate 7⅞ × 11 in.
Collection of the Tobin Endowment
Play by Prospero Bonarelli

Victor St. Léon
French, 1815–1870

Maquette for Act I, Scene 2 in *Semiramide*
Watercolor, ink, and graphite on cut paper mounted on board, 8½ × 12½ × 5 in.
Collection of the Tobin Endowment
Opera by Gioacchino Rossini

Tobin was not content simply to collect theatre arts. He had an educational mission as well. With longtime McNay theatre curator Linda Hardberger, Tobin organized an impressive series of landmark exhibitions, publications, and symposia. This tradition, which lives on at the McNay today, has involved visiting designers and scholars such as Desmond Heeley, Ming Cho Lee, John E. Bowlt, and Mary C. Henderson.

[12]

Tobin firmly believed that designs come to life only when they are used, and he wanted them to be accessible to students and scholars as well as to the general public. In particular, he hoped that his collection would educate and inspire young theatre designers. Every year professors and students from Texas universities, as well as international scholars, study the collection, conduct research in the library, and participate in special events.

The Tobin Collection continues to grow and to respond to emerging trends in theatre arts. Recent acquisitions include costume designs by the painters Edouard Vuillard, Alexandra Exter, and David Hockney. Artists who designed for the stage remain a primary focus, as do theatre designers who stand alongside visual artists as major stylistic innovators. In addition, as the collection moves into the twenty-first century, it will reflect ever new performance genres and design technologies.

Theatre brings together all the arts—literature, music, and dance as well as visual art. From medieval morality plays to Baroque operas to Broadway musicals, theatre has always been a powerful expression of the cultural, economic, political, religious, social, and technological issues of the time. As a key resource of the McNay, with its outstanding collection of modern and contemporary art, the Tobin Collection aims to further the interdisciplinary study of the arts.

Alexandra Exter
Russian, 1882–1949

Costume design for a female character in *Dama Duende (The Phantom Lady)*, 1924
Watercolor, graphite, ink, and collage on paper, 22⅜ × 16⅜ in.
Gift of the Tobin Foundation for Theatre Arts
TL2003.1
Play by Pedro Calderón de la Barca

David Hockney
British, born 1937

Costume designs for Columbine in *Parade*, 1980
Crayon, colored pencil, graphite, and gouache on paper, 22 × 24¼ in.
Gift of the Tobin Foundation for Theatre Arts
TL2003.2
Ballet with music by Erik Satie and choreography by Léonide Massine

LIBER QVINTVS

ROTVNDARV MONOP/
TERARVM:AC PERIP/
TERORVM AEDIVM IN
SVMO THOLATA FERE
PER INDICATA FIGVRA.

THEATRORVM INTVS
ET EXTRA ORTHO/
GRAPHIA, SCAENARV
POSTERIORVQ3 PORTI/
CARVM ICHNOGRAPHIA

RARE BOOKS AND
PAST PERFORMANCES

Rare books have been the foundation of the Tobin Collection of Theatre Arts since its inception. Robert L. B. Tobin began his theatre collection in the early 1950s, while a student at the University of Texas, by acquiring *Monumenta Scenica,* a twelve-volume compendium of seventeenth- and eighteenth-century European theatre design. Three decades later, he conceived of the Tobin Wing at the McNay as a grand library and gallery for original scene and costume designs. When this dramatic space was dedicated in March 1984, Tobin's first theatre gift to the museum included the rare books that fill its floor-to-ceiling bookcases.

Conceptually, rare books also provide a basis for the original scene and costume designs in the Tobin Collection. From ancient tragedies and medieval mystery plays to the commedia dell'arte and romantic ballets, much of our knowledge of Western theatre design before the twentieth century comes from illustrated books. The Tobin Collection has especially notable strengths in the areas of festival books, architectural treatises, and costume studies from the fifteenth through the nineteenth centuries.

Festival books commemorated European courtly celebrations such as weddings and coronations, politically important occasions that were observed with ceremonial processions, allegorical tableaux, and mock battles on both land and water. These elaborate events required settings, costumes, and special effects such as waterworks and pyrotechnics, all provided by court artists. The complex iconography and ostentatious display of these spectacles, which still fascinate today, were recorded in festival books created as souvenir gifts for invited dignitaries.

Illustration of a Roman theatre from Marcus Vitruvius Pollio, *De Architectura,* edited by Cesare Cesariano
Woodcut, image 5¾ × 5⅝ in.
Como, Italy: Gotardus de Ponte, 1521
Gift of Robert L. B. Tobin, TL1984.1.290

RIGHT
Robert L. B. Tobin and Linda Hardberger, curator of the Tobin Collection of Theatre Arts, prepare rare books for the opening of the Tobin Wing at the McNay Art Museum, 1984.

Remigio Cantagallina
Italian, 1582–1656

The Barge of Jason from *L'Argonautica*, 1608
Etching, plate 7⅝ × 10½ in.
Gift of Robert L. B. Tobin.
TL1990.13.7.1

Ferdinando Galli Bibiena
Italian, 1657–1743

Illustration of a scene design from *Direzioni della Prospettiva Teorica, Corrispondenti a quelle dell'Architettura*
Etching, plate 5⅜ × 5⅞ in.
Bologna, Italy: Stamperia di Lelio dalla Volpe, 1753
Gift of Robert L. B. Tobin, TL1984.1.273.2

 8

Illustration of a costume design for Chinese Emperor in Friedrich Schiller's *Turandot*, from *Kostum auf den Kon: National-Theater in Berlin*
Etching with hand coloring, plate 10⅛ × 5⅞ in.
Berlin: L. W. Wittich, 1808
Gift of Robert L. B. Tobin
TL1984.1.38.2

 9

Auguste Guillaumot Fils
French, 1844–1890
after Louis Boulanger, French, 1806–1867

Illustration of a costume design for Esméralda from Victor Hugo, *La Esméralda*
Etching with hand coloring, plate 9¼ × 7 in.
Paris: Emile Testard, 1888
Gift of Robert L. B. Tobin, TL1984.1.400

As courtly performances moved into specialized spaces, architects and historians sought to reconstruct the theatre settings of the Greek and Roman past. In addition, theorists and practitioners applied the principles of Renaissance and Baroque linear perspective to theatre architecture and scene painting. Perspective not only created the illusion of depth on the theatre stage but also reinforced social hierarchy in the audience through the privileged viewing position of aristocratic patrons.

During the period of neoclassicism and romanticism, ballet and opera, like other artistic genres, tended to emphasize historicism and exoticism. Illustrated surveys of period and regional costume were essential resources for designers in Europe and America in the nineteenth century. Books devoted to notable performers and productions of the day recorded theatre designers' variously accurate or fantastic portrayals of ancient gods, medieval maidens, and oriental rulers.

OPERAS CLASSIC AND CONTEMPORARY

pera was Robert L. B. Tobin's first love and the performance genre to which he was most devoted as a theatre patron and collector. Perhaps it was the heightened emotions of the music drama that attracted him to opera, or the sheer scale, overt artifice, and utter theatricality of the set and costume designs. Revealing in this respect are remarks that Tobin made on the occasion of the 1991 bicentennial of Mozart's birth. In the catalogue to the McNay's exhibition *Entirely Mozart,* Tobin explained the source of his admiration:

> The phenomenal effect of the composer [resides in] his ability to enrapture audiences, and above all, to move the spirit—that requires a suspension of belief that what has happened, what is happening, actually took, is taking, place.[1]

Set and costume designs for Mozart's *Così fan tutte, Don Giovanni, The Marriage of Figaro,* and *The Magic Flute* abound in the Tobin Collection. Also well represented are classics by Gluck, Massenet, Puccini, Rossini, Strauss, Verdi, and Wagner, all of which share themes of love and death, the exotic and the supernatural. From meticulous archaeological reconstructions to haunting surrealist dreamscapes to stark abstract environments, the designs in the Tobin Collection are indicative of the range of painterly styles in evidence in nineteenth- and twentieth-century European and American opera houses.

note 1. Robert L. B. Tobin, "Introduction," in *Entirely Mozart,* exh. cat. (San Antonio, Tex.: McNay Art Museum, 1991), p. 7.

10
Paul Knauerhase
German, 1858–1942

Scene design for Temple of Isis in *Die Zauberflote (The Magic Flute),* 1904
Watercolor and graphite on paper,
13⅝ × 19½ in.
Gift of the Tobin Endowment
TL2002.136
Opera by Wolfgang Amadeus Mozart

Enrico d'Assia
Italian, born 1927

Scene design for Act III, Scene 2 in *Turandot*, ca. 1965
Gouache, watercolor, and graphite on paper, 6½ × 11 in.
Gift of the Tobin Endowment
TL2002.70.1
Opera by Giacomo Puccini

Robert Wilson
American, born 1944

Scene design for Act I, Scene 1 in *Alceste*, 1986
Lithograph, image 21⅛ × 33⅛ in.
Gift of Robert L. B. Tobin
TL1999.382.2
Opera by Christoph Willibald Gluck

The collection extends far beyond the "standards." Indeed, Tobin was a champion of the contemporary repertoire and collected designs for a remarkable number of American premieres. These included Alberto Ginastera's *Bomarzo,* designed by Ming Cho Lee and José Varona for the Washington Opera Society, and Philip Glass's *Akhnaten,* designed by Robert Israel for the Würtenberger State Opera, Stuttgart. These twentieth-century operas addressed issues in modern society or presented contemporary interpretations of history, and the scores were often challenging musically as well as thematically.

13

Ming Cho Lee
American, born China, 1930

Scene design for The Inner Spirit in *Bomarzo*, 1967
Watercolor, ink, and graphite on paper,
5⅛ × 9⅜ in.
Gift of Robert L. B. Tobin
TL1999.156
Opera by Alberto Ginastera

14

Robert Israel
American, born 1939

Costume design for Nefertiti in Coronation Gown, Act II in *Akhnaten*, 1992
Watercolor and ink on paper, 29⅞ × 22¼ in.
Gift of Robert L. B. Tobin
TL1999.88.19
Opera by Philip Glass

SHAKESPEAREAN STAGES FROM BRITAIN TO AMERICA

Designs for Shakespeare's tragedies, histories, and comedies are an exception to the Tobin Collection's emphasis on musical theatre. In English-speaking countries, "the Bard" is still among the first playwrights encountered by theatre students and theatregoers alike. Tobin described the implications of this familiarity on theatre design:

> The plot is firmly in place, negating the necessity of the director and designer to convey basic information—only to comment on it. The freedom this gives is virtually unlimited and is as much of a challenge as it is an asset.[1]

At the McNay, pride of place is given to British designers for Shakespeare, but Tobin also collected the work of German designers influential in the early twentieth century. Designs by Percy Macquoid for *The Winter's Tale,* directed by Herbert Beerbohm Tree at Her Majesty's Theatre, and by W. Graham Robertson for *Richard II* exemplify the antiquarianism of Victorian and Edwardian theatre. The broader treatment of Adolf Hengeler's costume design for *The Merchant of Venice,* directed by Max Reinhardt at the Deutsches Theater, Berlin, provides quite a contrast. Adolf Linnebach's scene design for *Hamlet* at the Dresden State Theatre, which relies more on atmospheric lighting than on painterly detail, is also indicative of the departure from pictorial illusionism characteristic of the New Stagecraft.

Tobin had a particular interest in the neo-romantic painters who emerged in France and Great Britain in the mid-1930s. In 1938, John Gielgud invited the young artists Michael Ayrton and John Minton to design a production of *Macbeth* at the Piccadilly Theatre in London. The distorted perspectives and ruinous grandeur of the settings betray the influence of the neo-romantics Eugene Berman, Christian Bérard, and Pavel Tchelitchev, whom Ayrton and Minton knew in Paris.

note 1. Robert L. B. Tobin, "Introduction," in *Twentieth-Century British Stage Design*, exh. cat. (San Antonio, Tex.: McNay Art Museum, 1993), pp. 6–7.

15
Percy Macquoid
British, 1852–1925

Costume design for Ellen Terry as Hermione in *The Winter's Tale,* 1906
Ink, watercolor, metallic paint, and graphite on board, 11⅝ × 9⅛ in.
Gift of the Tobin Endowment
TL2002.152.21

Dresses 2 & 3 same cut.

tone of blue.

shoes silver with diamonds.

Forming also veil
over dress. grey crepe de chine
very thin — silver fringe at
bottom, blue wave pattern
under dress. silver & blue thin
stuff (Hunter) sleeves of grey Chiffon
as if an under dress
    same Tiara
diamond buttons on sleeve

— HERMOINE —
  dress 2 Trial scene
    and in white
crepe de chine for Act. 5
all white to imitate a statue
  sleeves of course here
      not transparent.

The ornament a base of skirt
is a cube square of light colored
sapphires sewn on separately, each
square in a square of same size
       & a half apart.

16

Adolf Hengeler
German, 1863–1927

Costume design for Shylock in *The Merchant of Venice*, 1905
Graphite, ink, watercolor, and fabric swatches on paper, 12¼ × 12¾ in.
Gift of the Tobin Endowment
TL2002.101

17

Adolf Linnebach
German, 1876–1963

Scene design for Parapet in *Hamlet*, 1907
Watercolor, ink, and graphite on paper, 8¼ × 11⅞ in.
Gift of the Tobin Endowment
TL2002.151.1

18

Michael Ayrton
British, 1921–1975

Costume design for a Messenger, Act I, Scene 5
in *Macbeth*, 1941
Gouache, graphite, and ink on paper, 11 × 7¼ in.
Gift of the Tobin Endowment
TL2002.28.2

19

John Minton
British, 1917–1957

Scene design for Act V, Scenes 1 and 3 in *Macbeth*, 1938
Ink, watercolor, and graphite on paper, 9 × 11½ in.
Gift of the Tobin Endowment
TL2002.167.2

20

Tanya Moiseiwitsch
British, 1914–2003

Costume design for Queen Elizabeth in *Richard III*, 1953
Gouache, ink, watercolor, and metallic paint on paper, 14⅞ × 12 in.
Gift of the Tobin Endowment
TL2002.176

21

Leslie Hurry
British, 1909–1978

View of the stage for *King Lear* at the Stratford Festival, 1964
Watercolor, graphite, and ink on paper, 7³⁄₁₆ × 10⅝ in.
Gift of the Tobin Endowment
TL2002.108.4

In North America the creative collaboration between director Tyrone Guthrie and designer Tanya Moiseiwitsch was one of the most influential in the post–Second World War era. At the Stratford Festival, established in Ontario, Canada, in 1953, they realized their idea to present Shakespeare in a setting recalling the Elizabethan architectural stage rather than the nineteenth-century proscenium stage. In this spare and neutral environment, costumes became major dramatic and scenic elements, conveying meaning, establishing character, and creating visual impact. Moiseiwitsch, Desmond Heeley, and Leslie Hurry, who all designed extensively for the Stratford Festival, are well represented in the Tobin Collection.

EDWARD GORDON CRAIG'S NEW STAGECRAFT

Edward Gordon Craig was a giant of modern scene design, as important to twentieth-century theatre as Cézanne or Gauguin were to modern painting. Craig, son of the actress Ellen Terry, was one of the pioneers of the so-called New Stagecraft in Europe and America. This movement entailed an antinaturalistic reform of the nineteenth-century stage, favoring abstraction and expressiveness over mimetic representation. Because of the revolutionary nature of Craig's vision, as well as personality conflicts and technical difficulties, his designs were rarely produced. Craig's collaboration with Konstantin Stanislavsky on a notorious production of *Hamlet* at the Moscow Art Theatre in 1911 was a notable exception. Regardless, Craig's ideas exerted a profound influence in Europe and America.

Tobin assembled an extraordinary collection of Craig's work, including manuscripts, books, drawings, prints, and scale models. Craig outlined his ideas for a sculptural and illuminated space as opposed to an illusionistic and painted space in visionary publications such as *Towards a New Theatre* (1913). In scene designs for *Hamlet* and *Macbeth,* Craig sought to realize this vision by means of folding screens and modular blocks. Most remarkably, he created scale models of the screens and blocks as well as of the actors. The expressive silhouettes of these balsa wood figures exemplified Craig's notion of the actor as a "super puppet."

22

Edward Gordon Craig
British, 1872–1966

Scene design for *Hamlet,* 1905
Crayon, watercolor, chalk, and ink on paper, 21 × 17½ in.
Gift of the Tobin Endowment
TL2002.56.1

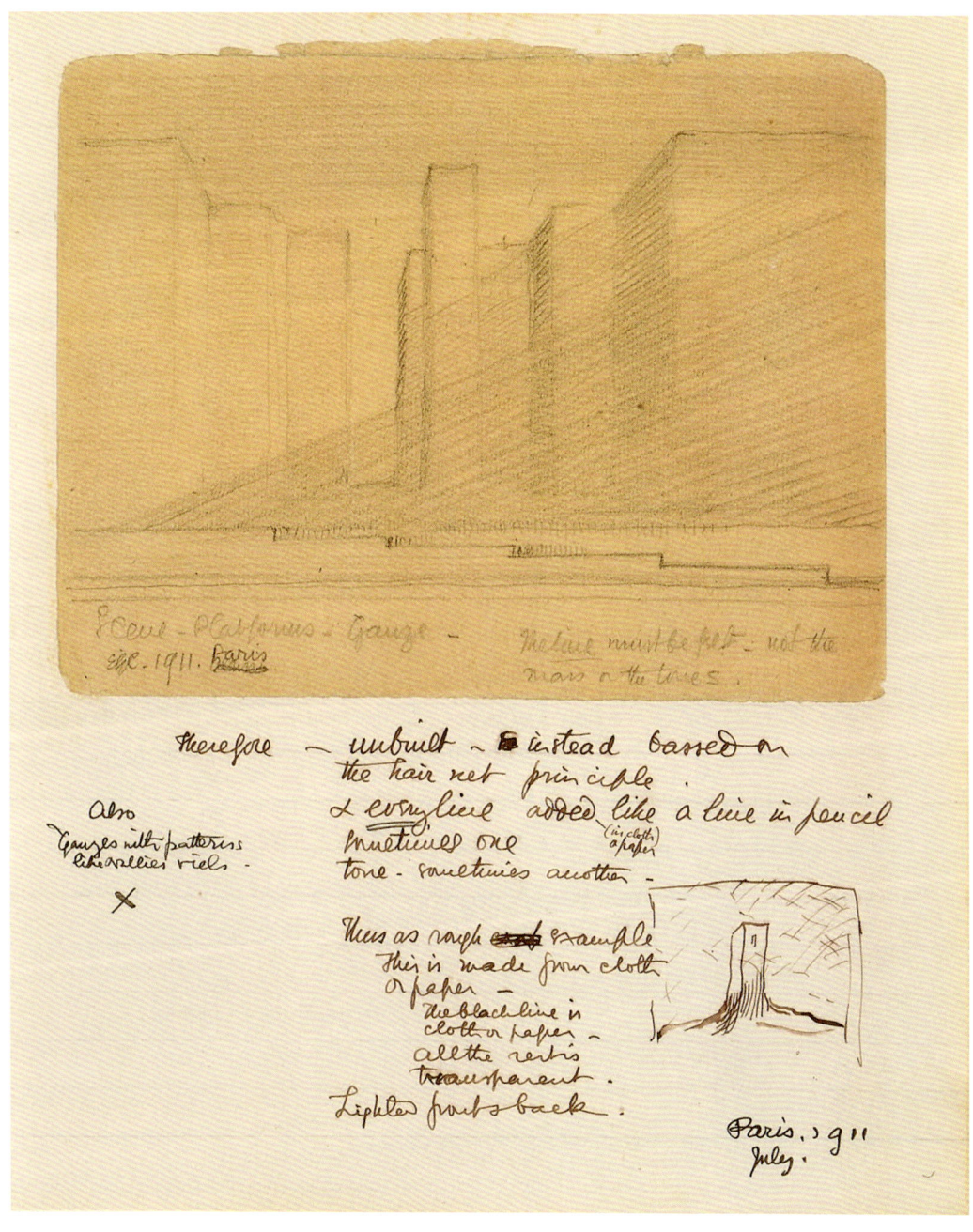

23
Edward Gordon Craig
British, 1872–1966

Scene design for Hamlet Greeting the Actors,
Act III in *Hamlet,* 1926
Watercolor and pastel on paper, 18 × 22½ in.
Gift of Margaret Batts Tobin
TL1988.1.258

24
Edward Gordon Craig
British, 1872–1966

Model for Screens with Black Figure: Hamlet
Greeting the Actors, ca. 1907
Paper on board with linen hinges; wood
engraving on board; screens: 17⅝ in. high and
11¾ in. high; black figure: 2⅜ in. high
Gift of Robert L. B. Tobin
TL1984.1.1066.1, 4

25
Edward Gordon Craig
British, 1872–1966

Preliminary scene design for *Macbeth,* 1911
Graphite on paper, 6 × 4⅝ in.
Gift of the Tobin Endowment
TL2002.58.2

OUT OF RUSSIA

26
Léon Bakst
Russian, 1866–1924

Costume design for an Odalisque in *Schéhérazade*, 1911
Gouache, graphite, ink, and metallic paint on paper mounted on board, 17 11/16 × 11 13/16 in.
Gift of Robert L. B. Tobin
TL1999.2
Ballet with music by Nikolai Rimsky-Korsakov and choreography by Michel Fokine

Explosion: Color: Paris: 1909 is the title that Tobin gave to an exhibition devoted to Serge Diaghilev's Ballets Russes at the McNay Art Museum in 1969. According to Tobin, "There had never been anything like the Russian Ballet and there never will be again."[1] For many, the Tobin Collection is synonymous with the Russian artists who, beginning in 1908–9, captivated and exhilarated Western European audiences with the exotic themes and vibrant color of their designs for ballet and opera.

Russia's leading artists were eager to collaborate with Diaghilev and his talented composers and choreographers in this pathbreaking interdisciplinary endeavor. Their designs effectively swept away the mediocrity of nineteenth-century stock scenery and costumes. The Ballets Russes became a catalyst for modernist experiments in synthesizing the visual and the performing arts in Europe and America.

The Tobin Collection includes important examples of the major phases in Russian scene design for Diaghilev's Ballets Russes and other theatre companies in Russia and the West. In the first decade of the twentieth century, Léon Bakst and Alexandre Benois exemplified the symbolist tendencies of *Mir Iskusstva* (World of Art). This movement, centered in St. Petersburg, was known for fairy-tale romanticism, exotic escapism, and coloristic exuberance.

On the eve of the First World War, Moscow-based artists Natalia Gontcharova and Mikhail Larionov created designs that reflected their love of Russian folk arts and their interest in the stylistic vocabularies of cubo-futurism. After the Russian Revolution in 1917, constructivists such as Alexandra Exter and Liubov Popova sought to create an antibourgeois art by utilizing modern engineering materials and proletarian aesthetics for set and costume designs.

note   1. Robert L. B. Tobin, "Bakst/Benois," in *Bakst and Benois*, exh. cat. (San Antonio, Tex.: McNay Art Museum, 1993), p. 7.

27
Alexandre Benois
Russian, 1870–1960

Preliminary scene design for Act I in *Giselle*, 1910
Watercolor and ink on paper, 6⅞ × 10⅜ in.
Gift of Robert L. B. Tobin
TL1998.103.1
Ballet with music by Adolphe Adam and choreography by Jean Coralli and Jules Perrot

28
Alexandre Benois
Russian, 1870–1960

Scene design for the King's Bedroom, Act III in *Le Rossignol (The Nightingale)*, 1914
Gouache, pastel, and paper mounted on canvas, 38⅝ × 42⁷⁄₁₆ in.
Gift of Robert L. B. Tobin
TL1998.111
Opera by Igor Stravinsky

29
Pavel Tchelitchev
Russian, 1898–1957

Costume designs for *Coucher du Soleil (Sunset),* ca. 1919
Gouache, watercolor, and graphite on paper, 12 × 18¼ in.
Gift of Robert L. B. Tobin
TL1998.346

30
Mikhail Larionov
Russian, 1881–1964

Costume design for La Femme du Vieux Bouffon (Wife of the Old Buffoon) in *Chout (The Buffoon),* ca. 1921
Watercolor and charcoal on board, 14½ × 9⅝ in.
Gift of Robert L. B. Tobin
TL1998.263
Ballet with music by Serge Prokofiev and choreography by Tadeusz Slavinsky and Mikhail Larionov

[39]

31

Liubov Popova
Russian, 1889–1924

Preliminary scene design for *The Magnanimous Cuckold*, ca. 1920–22
Gouache, ink, and graphite on paper, 6¼ × 10¼ in.
Gift of the Tobin Endowment
TL2001.108
Play by Fernand Crommelynck

32

Alexandra Exter
Russian, 1882–1949

Costume design for a female character in *Aelita: Queen of Mars*, 1924
Gouache, ink, and graphite on paper, 19 × 12⅞ in.
Gift of the Tobin Endowment
TL2001.61
Film directed by Yakov Protazanov

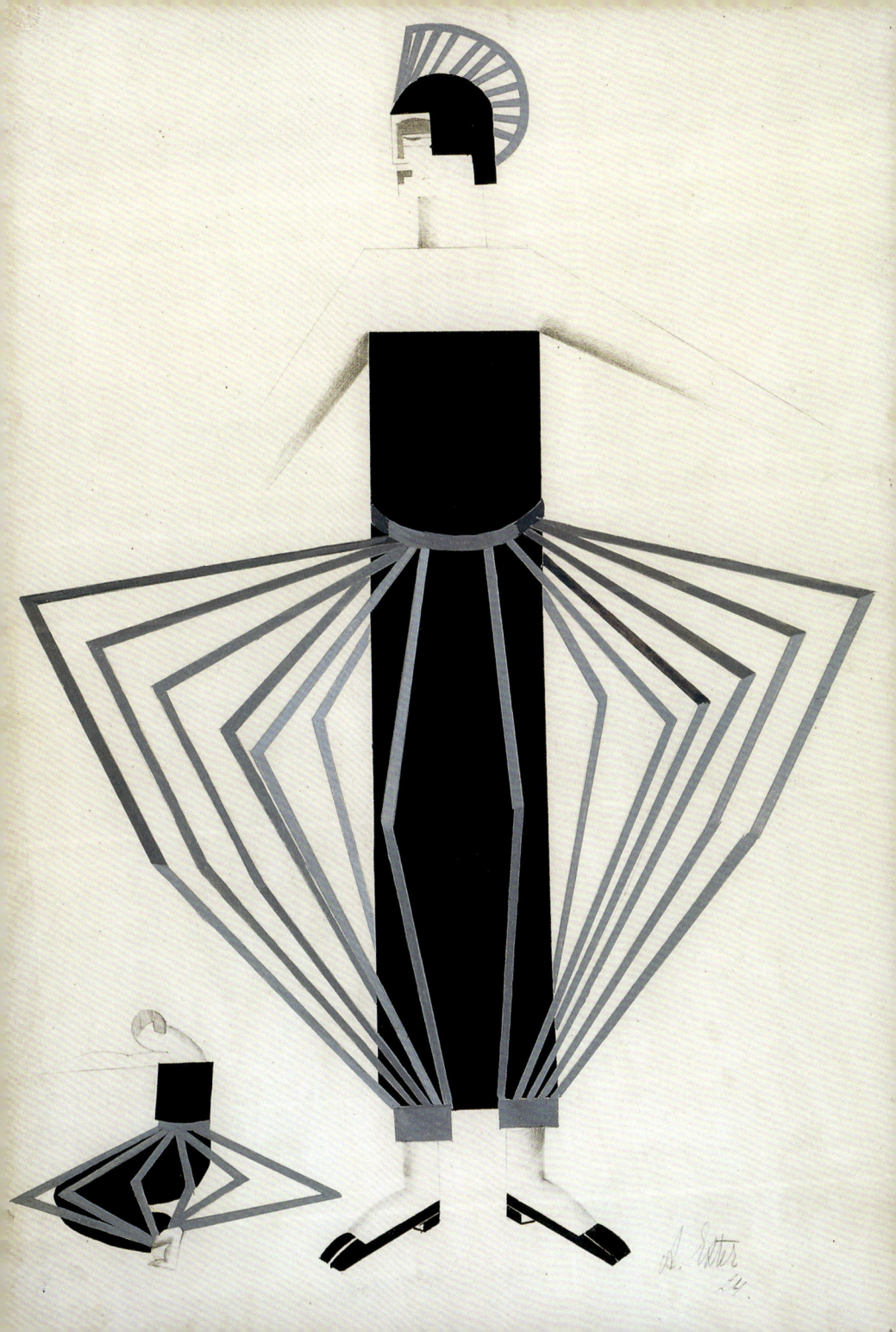

NATALIA GONTCHAROVA: FOLKLORE AND FINE ART

Among the artists working for the Ballets Russes, Natalia Gontcharova was Tobin's personal favorite. Gontcharova designed extensively for Diaghilev's company and, after Diaghilev's death in 1929, for the Ballets Russes de Colonel de Basil. Her scene and costume designs for *Le Coq d'or (The Golden Cockerel),* by Rimsky-Korsakov and Michel Fokine, helped to make the ballet one of Diaghilev's great successes. Based on a folk tale published by Alexander Pushkin about an incompetent czar, *Le Coq d'or* was revived by de Basil in 1937 with additional costumes and drops by Gontcharova.

A constant in Gontcharova's wide-ranging work—from painting, collage, and printmaking to book illustration and scene design—was her fascination with folk art. This included the popular religious icons of her native Russia and the rich textile designs of Spain, where Diaghilev's company was based during the First World War. Gontcharova drew on these sources in her designs for *Liturgie* and several ballets with Spanish themes that, unfortunately, were never produced.

Gontcharova's style evolved along with trends in European modernism. In the teens, she created distinct versions of primitivism, exemplified by the bright colors and simplified shapes of *Le Coq d'or,* and cubo-futurism, apparent in the angular geometry of *Liturgie* and the shifting planes of the *Spanish Dancer.* After the war, Gontcharova returned to a more naturalistic style in decorative panels and book illustrations inspired by Rimsky-Korsakov's *Snow Maiden* and Pushkin's *Tsar Saltan.*

Robert Tobin with Natalia Gontcharova's painting of General Polkan from *Le Coq d'or (The Golden Cockerel)* (ca. 1922), at the Grolier Club, New York City, 1983.

33

Natalia Gontcharova
Russian, 1881–1962

Scene design for Act I in *Le Coq d'or (The Golden Cockerel)*, 1913
Watercolor, gouache, graphite on paper, 12¼ × 16 in.
Gift of Robert L. B. Tobin
TL1998.173
Opera-ballet with music by Nikolai Rimsky-Korsakov and choreography by Michel Fokine

34

Natalia Gontcharova
Russian, 1881–1962

Costume design for the Old Woman of the Keys in *Le Coq d'or (The Golden Cockerel)*, ca. 1914
Watercolor and gouache on paper, 13¼ × 10 in.
Gift of Robert L. B. Tobin
TL1999.6

35

Natalia Gontcharova
Russian, 1881–1962

Spanish Dancer, 1916
Gouache, collage, watercolor, and graphite on board, 29¾ × 21 in.
Gift of Robert L. B. Tobin
TL1998.233

36

Natalia Gontcharova
Russian, 1881–1962

Costume design for an Apostle in *Liturgie,* 1915
Watercolor on board, 18¾ × 11⅞ in.
Gift of Robert L. B. Tobin
TL1998.191
Unrealized ballet conceived by Léonide Massine

37

Natalia Gontcharova
Russian, 1881–1962

Winter in *The Snow Maiden,* ca. 1922
Oil on canvas, 91¼ × 39½ in.
Gift of Robert L. B. Tobin
TL1998.205

FROM STUDIOS TO STAGES
IN MODERNIST PARIS

Pablo Picasso
Spanish, 1881–1973

Maquette for *Le Tricorne (The Three-Cornered Hat)*, 1919
Watercolor and graphite on board, 6¼ × 10½ × 5½ in.
Gift of the Tobin Endowment
TL2001.105
Ballet with music by Manuel de Falla and choreography by Léonide Massine

Henri Matisse
French, 1869–1954

Cape for the Emperor in *Le Chant du Rossignol (The Song of the Nightingale)*, 1920
Silk with metallic embroidery and studs
Gift of the Tobin Endowment
TL2001.92
Ballet with music by Igor Stravinsky and choreography by Léonide Massine

During the First World War and after the Russian Revolution, Diaghilev turned increasingly to Paris-based artists, among them many international expatriates. In the late teens and twenties, designing for the Ballets Russes was a sign of artistic status in the cosmopolitan Paris art world. Henri Matisse, known for his love of pattern, and Pablo Picasso, proud of his Catalan heritage, were obvious choices to design ballets that continued the Ballets Russes' ongoing fascination with oriental or Spanish settings.

Rivals to and successors of Diaghilev's Ballets Russes, Rolf de Maré's Ballets Suédois and the Ballets Russes de Monte Carlo continued the tradition of engaging modernist artists in theatre design. Fernand Léger's designs for *Création du monde (Creation of the World)*, composed by Darius Milhaud, and Giorgio de Chirico's designs for *Protée (Proteus)*, choreographed to music by Claude Debussy, exemplified interest after the First World War in cultural renewal, manifested in references to creation myths of Africa and Greece.

40

Fernand Léger
French, 1881–1955

Costume designs for animals in *Création du Monde (Creation of the World)*, ca. 1923
Gouache and ink on paper, 8 11/16 × 10 15/16 in.
Gift of the Tobin Endowment
TL2001.88.2
Ballet with music by Darius Milhaud and choreography by Jean Börlin

41

Giorgio de Chirico
Italian, born Greece, 1888–1978

Costume design for Brigelle dressed as a man in *Protée (Proteus)*, 1938
Watercolor and graphite on paper, 12 × 10 in.
Gift of the Tobin Endowment
TL2001.47.4
Ballet with music by Claude Debussy and choreography by David Lichine

42 | 43

Sonia Delaunay
Russian, 1885–1979

Costume designs for Bride and Groom in *La Coeur à gaz (The Gas-Operated Heart)*, 1923
Lithograph, sheets 17½ × 8⅜ in. and 17¾ × 8⅜ in.
Gift of the Tobin Endowment
TL2001.49.2, 4
Play by Tristan Tzara

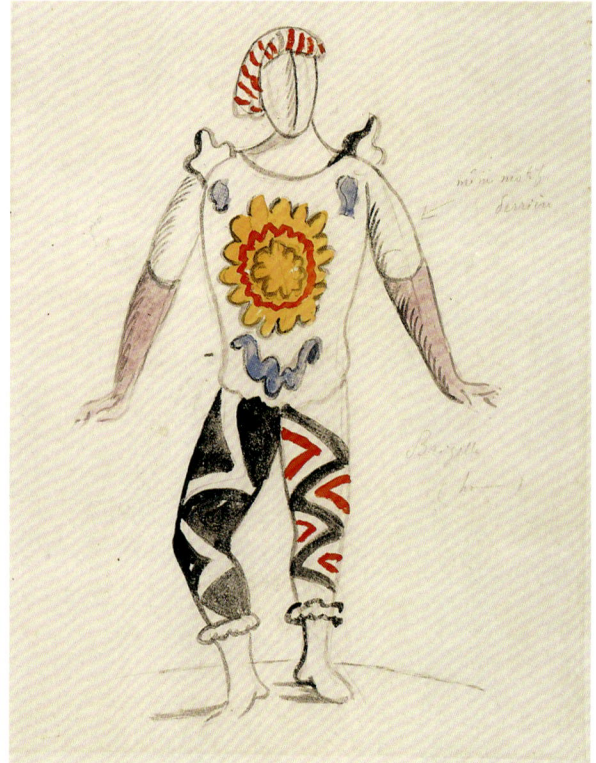

The Dadaists sought to break away from traditional artistic media and to bridge the gap between high art and everyday life by means of performance. *La Coeur à gaz (The Gas-Operated Heart)*, a provocative and nonsensical play written by Tristan Tzara, was billed as the only and greatest three-act hoax of the century. It featured witty cardboard costumes designed by painter Sonia Delaunay for characters that included Nose and Mouth as well as Bride and Groom.

14/25. Sonia Delaunay

14/25 Sonia Delaunay

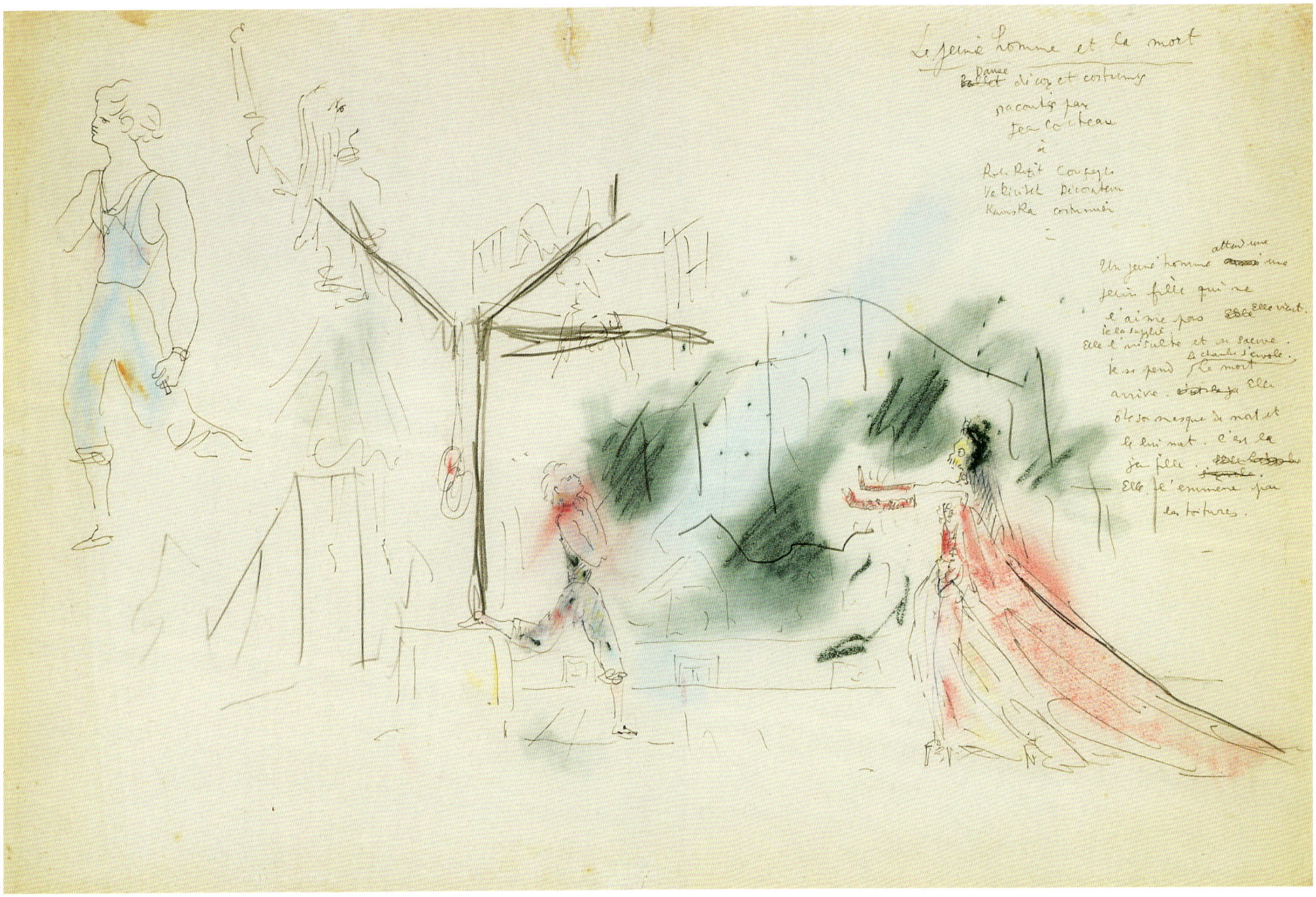

Jean Cocteau
French, 1889–1963

Scene design for *Le Jeune Homme et la Mort*
(*The Young Man and Death*), 1946
Graphite, pastel, and ink on paper, 13¼ × 19¾ in.
Gift of the Tobin Endowment
TL2001.40
Ballet with music by Johann Sebastian Bach
and choreography by Roland Petit

Leonor Fini
French, born Argentina, 1908

Costume designs for Musician and Cats in *Les
Demoiselles de la nuit* (*The Women of the Night*),
ca. 1948
Ink and gouache on paper, 12¹³⁄₁₆ × 9¹³⁄₁₆ in.
Gift of the Tobin Endowment
TL2002.74
Ballet with music by Jean Françaix and
choreography by Roland Petit

R oland Petit, protégé of Ballets Russes choreographer Serge Lifar, formed his own ballet companies in Paris in the mid- to late 1940s. In the climate of surrealism, he produced *Les Demoiselles de la nuit (The Women of the Night)*, with designs by painter Leonor Fini, and *Le Jeune Homme et la Mort (The Young Man and Death)*, with designs by writer and filmmaker Jean Cocteau. Both ballets deal with the mythical connections between genius and madness, and between love and death, familiar themes from the surrealist novels of André Breton or the paintings of Salvador Dalí.

EUGENE BERMAN, NEO-ROMANTIC

In the early 1950s Tobin made his first acquisition of theatre arts: scene and costume designs for *Rigoletto* by Russian émigré draftsman, painter, and sculptor Eugene Berman. The first exhibition in the McNay's newly opened Tobin Wing in March 1984 was *Eugene Berman and the Theatre of Melancholia*. In the catalogue, Tobin stated:

> If Eugene Berman casts a shadow on the twentieth century scene, it will quite certainly be one of the mysterious melancholia, the obsession…not so much with the actual past but an imaginary past, full of theatrical devices and allusions.[1]

Robert Tobin and Margaret Tobin with maquette by Eugene Berman in Spoleto, Italy, 1966.

Tobin initiated a lifelong friendship with Berman, to which he attributed much of his appreciation of theatre design. Tobin loved Mozart's operas, which Berman designed extensively, and he shared Berman's taste for the neo-romantic. This was manifested in a preference for overwhelming architectural scale and mysterious natural light as well as nostalgia for ruins and a fascination with the macabre.

Berman and fellow Russian Pavel Tchelitchev, along with Frenchman Christian Bérard, were the nucleus of the neo-romantic painters in Paris between the wars. All three became involved with theatre design for the ballet troupes that competed for Diaghilev's legacy after the impresario's death. They put as much of a visual stamp on the choreography of Massine and Balanchine as Diaghilev's designers had on the choreography of Fokine and Nijinsky.

The Ballets Russes de Colonel de Basil brought Berman to the United States, where he continued to pursue his career as a painter, exhibiting at the Julien Levy Gallery in New York City, and as a designer. Berman was one of the most important designers at the Metropolitan Opera under the directorship of Rudolf Bing. His productions included *Rigoletto, Don Giovanni, La Forza del Destino,* and *Otello.*

note 1. Robert L.B. Tobin, in *Eugene Berman and the Theatre of Melancholia,* exh. cat. (San Antonio, Tex.: McNay Art Museum, 1984), p. 7.

46

Eugene Berman
American, born Russia, 1899–1972

Costume design for Giselle, Act I in *Giselle*, 1946
Ink and watercolor on paper, 12⅜ × 9 in.
Gift of the Tobin Endowment
TL2001.25.6
Ballet with music by Adolphe Adam and choreography by Anton Dolin after Jean Coralli and Jules Perrot

47

Eugene Berman
American, born Russia, 1899–1972

Scene design for *Danses Concertantes*
Watercolor and ink on paper, 8¾ × 12⅜ in.
Gift of the Tobin Endowment
TL2001.20
Ballet with music by Igor Stravinsky and choreography by George Balanchine

𝓘n *Eugene Berman and the Theatre of Melancholia,* Tobin observed that Berman's designs for Verdi's *La Forza del Destino (The Power of Fate)* at the Metropolitan Opera were typical of the liberties he took with historical setting. In Tobin's opinion, this production included "one memorable scene, probably the most Bermanesque of his lifetime: the battle-field was set with disintegrating columns against a ruined colosseum hovering under a green sky."[2]

note   2. Ibid., p. 10.

48

Eugene Berman
American, born Russia, 1899–1972

Backdrop design for Act II, Scene 5 (Finale) in *Don Giovanni*, 1957
Watercolor, ink, and graphite on paper, 10¼ × 15 in.
Gift of the Tobin Endowment
TL2001.22.48
Opera by Wolfgang Amadeus Mozart

49

Eugene Berman
American, born Russia, 1899–1972

Maquette for Act II in *La Forza del Destino (The Power of Fate)*, 1952
Watercolor and ink on paper and board with found objects, 10⅛ × 16⅛ × 8¹¹⁄₁₆ in.
Gift of the Tobin Endowment
TL2002.24.2
Opera by Giuseppe Verdi

THE GOLDEN AGE OF
THE BROADWAY MUSICAL

The musical is one of the United States' distinctive art forms. Its origins can be traced to the nineteenth century and the merger of melodrama, ballet, and light opera. The Tobin Collection includes designs for productions that celebrate the origin and the development of the American musical genre. For example, *Girl in Pink Tights* (1954) commemorates the historic 1866 collaboration between a ballet company and a melodrama troupe. *George M!* (1968) pays tribute to the early twentieth-century songwriter and showman George M. Cohan.

The Tobin Collection is especially rich in materials related to the classic musicals of the period after the Second World War. These were often based on popular books and provided the basis for many a hit movie, becoming important keystones of postwar American culture. These productions involved legendary collaborations among composers, writers, directors, and choreographers, including such stellar groupings as Richard Rodgers and Oscar Hammerstein in *South Pacific* (1949); Leonard Bernstein, Jerome Robbins, and Stephen Sondheim in *West Side Story* (1957); and George Abbott, Jerome Lawrence, Robert E. Lee, and Jerry Herman in *Mame* (1966).

The success of such musicals also stemmed from the talents of some of the most prolific designers in Broadway history. Jo Mielziner, Oliver Smith, and Jean and William Eckart made a distinctive stylistic contribution to many of the notable American musicals from the 1940s to the 1960s. Mielziner demonstrated his coloristic brilliance in the opening street scene from *A Tree Grows in Brooklyn* (1951). Smith's spatial virtuosity is evident in the Cave of the Questing Beast in *Camelot* (1960). And there is no better example of the Eckarts' linear elegance than the show curtain for *Damn Yankees* (1955).

50
Jo Mielziner
American, born France, 1901–1976

Scene design for *A Tree Grows in Brooklyn*, 1951
Watercolor, ink, and graphite on board, 13½ × 24 in.
Gift of Robert L. B. Tobin
TL1999.202
Musical with lyrics by Dorothy Fields and music by Arthur Schwartz

51
Jo Mielziner
American, born France, 1901–1976

Design for transformation drop for Bali Ha'i in *South Pacific,* 1949
Watercolor on paper, 13⅛ × 22¼ in.
Gift of Robert L. B. Tobin
TL1999.200
Musical with lyrics by Oscar Hammerstein II and music by Richard Rodgers

52
Oliver Smith
American, 1918–1994

Scene design for Under the Highway in *West Side Story,* 1957
Watercolor and graphite on paper, 15¾ × 23 in.
Gift of Robert L. B. Tobin
TL1999.314
Musical with lyrics by Stephen Sondheim and music by Leonard Bernstein

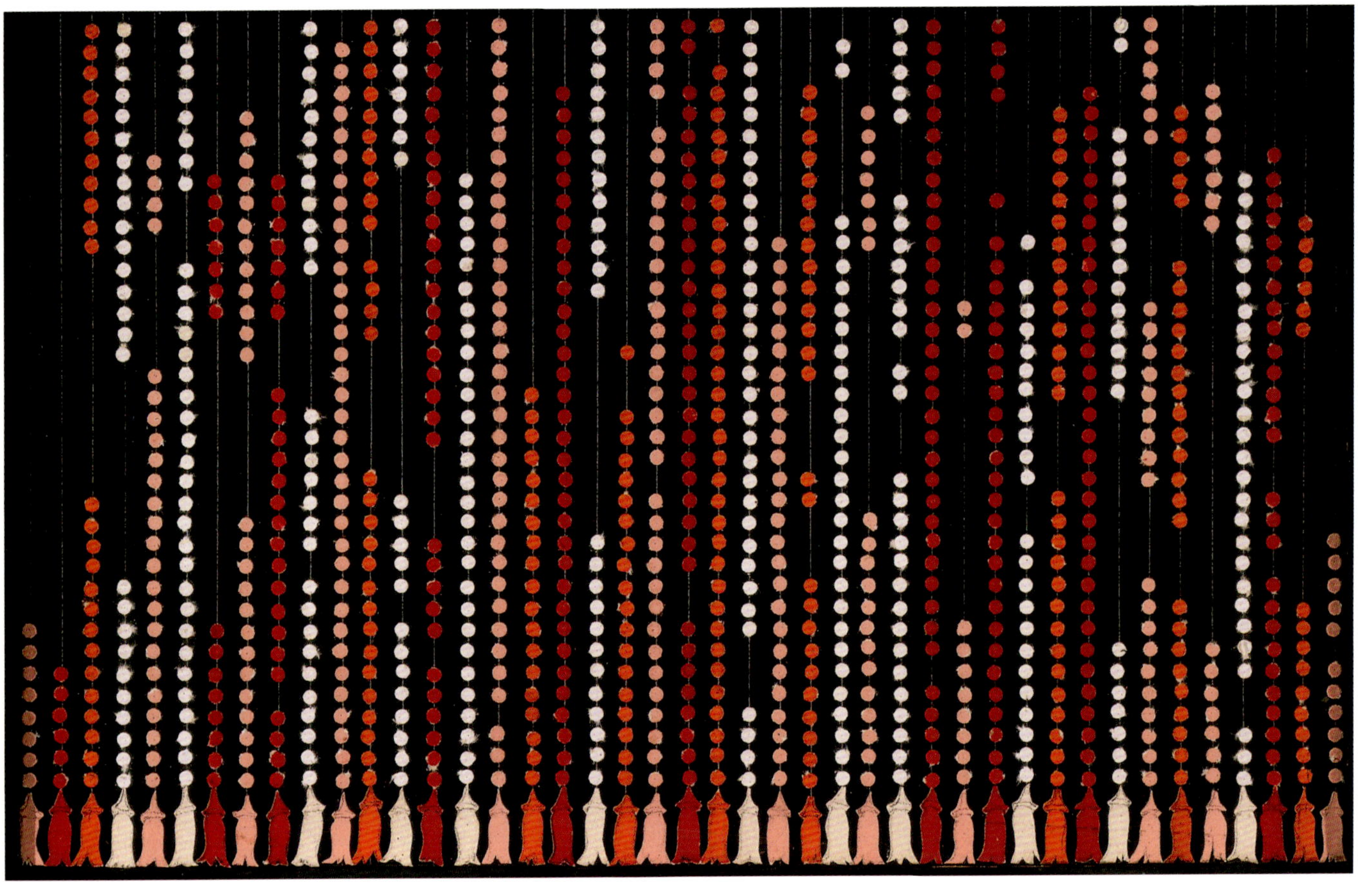

53
Jean Eckart
American, 1921–1994

William Eckart
American, 1921–2000

Curtain design for *Damn Yankees,* 1955
Collage and crayon on Mylar and paper,
9½ × 12½ in.
Gift of Robert L. B. Tobin
TL1999.66
Musical with lyrics and music by Richard Adler and Jerry Ross

54
Jean Eckart
American, 1921–1994

William Eckart
American, 1921–2000

Scene design for Open a New Window, Act I, Scene 5 in *Mame,* 1966
Crayon and graphite on layered paper,
7½ × 10 in.
Gift of Robert L. B. Tobin
TL1999.76.2
Musical with lyrics and music by Jerry Herman

55
Oliver Smith
American, 1918–1994

Scene design for Cave of the Questing Beast in *Camelot,* 1960
Watercolor and graphite on board, 8 × 11¾ in.
Gift of Robert L. B. Tobin
TL1999.297
Musical with lyrics by Alan Jay Lerner and music by Frederick Loewe

BALLETS AND OPERAS OF AMERICAN LIFE

Throughout the twentieth century, composers, choreographers, and librettists have come together to create distinctively American as opposed to European ballets and operas. Thematically, they have emphasized settings such as the immigrant city, the western frontier, or the rural south. Musically, they have incorporated vernacular idioms such as hoe-downs, marches, spirituals, and jazz. Choreographically, they have taken inspiration from the everyday movements of work and play or from popular dance genres.

Designers of settings and costumes for these ballets and operas of American life have employed visual languages that parallel key movements of twentieth-century American modernism. These styles range from the gritty realism of the Ash Can School, the formal abstraction of the Alfred Stieglitz circle, and the heroic figuration of American Scene painting to the saturated hues of color field painting and the mass-media imagery of Pop art.

56

Robert Edmond Jones
American, 1887–1954

Scene design for Steel Girders,
Scene 6 in *Skyscrapers,* 1926
Watercolor and ink on paper
with collage, 18 × 25½ in.
Gift of Robert L. B. Tobin
TL1999.116.1
Ballet with music by John Alden
and choreography by Sammy Lee

57

Robert Yodice
American, 1947–1983

Costume design for *Ellis Island*, 1976
Watercolor and graphite on paper,
20 × 16 in.
Gift of Robert L. B. Tobin
TL1999.397
Ballet with music by Charles Ives and choreography by Anna Sokolow

58

Adrianne Lobel
American, born 1955

Maquette for *Street Scene*, 1994
Painted board, plastic, and found objects,
16 × 25¾ × 23 in.
Gift of the Tobin Foundation for Theatre Arts
TL2002.11
Musical with lyrics by Langston Hughes and music by Kurt Weill

59
Oliver Smith
American, 1918–1994

Scene design for Act II in the revival of *Rodeo*, 1973
Watercolor and gouache on paper, 20½ × 34 in.
Gift of Robert L. B. Tobin
TL1999.307.1
Ballet with music by Aaron Copeland and choreography by Agnes de Mille

60
Franco Colavecchia
American, born 1937

Scene design for Voodoo, Act II, Scene 1 in *Treemonisha*, 1975
Watercolor and ink on paper, 12 × 19 in.
Gift of Robert L. B. Tobin
TL1999.57.4
Opera by Scott Joplin

ROBERT INDIANA: THE MOTHER OF US ALL

Robert Indiana (left) and Robert Tobin at the installation of *AHAVA (LOVE)* in Central Park, New York City, 1978.

The *Mother of Us All* is Gertrude Stein and Virgil Thomson's opera about Susan B. Anthony and women's suffrage. Thomson invited Pop artist Robert Indiana to design a revival of the 1947 opera at the Walker Art Center in Minneapolis in 1967. With backing from Robert Tobin, an important collector and friend of the artist, Indiana designed a more ambitious version at the Santa Fe Opera in 1976, which included a bicentennial procession during the overture.

Stein and Thomson first met in Paris in the mid-1920s. The composer believed that Stein's unconventional poems were closer to music than to speech, and he suggested that they collaborate. In *The Mother of Us All,* commissioned by Columbia University, Stein brought together characters from different times and places, creating an effect of simultaneity similar to that in the cubist paintings of Picasso, a close friend of the poet. Likewise, in his score for the opera, Thomson combined disparate elements—Protestant hymns, sentimental waltzes, and military marches—like found objects in a cubist collage.

Indiana, who incorporated aspects of popular American culture—from pinball machines to highway signs—in his paintings, prints, and sculptures, was an ideal artist to update *The Mother of Us All.* His final designs are paper cutouts, and the costumes and sets were executed in felt. He used these materials to achieve the bold colors, crisp edges, and shadowless surfaces of his Pop art paintings and prints. He also employed the stencil-style typography that was his artistic signature.

61

Robert Indiana
American, born 1928

Design for the Ship of State, Prow, Bicentennial Procession, Overture in *The Mother of Us All,* 1976
Cut paper, 30 × 20 in.
Gift of Robert L. B. Tobin
1978.11.46
Opera with lyrics by Gertrude Stein and music by Virgil Thomson

62

Robert Indiana
American, born 1928

Scene design for Drawing Room in the House
of Susan B. Anthony, Act II, Scenes 1 and 2
in *The Mother of Us All*, 1976
Cut paper, 28½ × 40 in.
Gift of Robert L. B. Tobin
1978.11.41

63

Robert Indiana
American, born 1928

Costume design for Susan B. Anthony
in *The Mother of Us All*, 1966–76
Cut paper, 26 × 20 in.
Gift of Robert L. B. Tobin
1978.12.4

64

Robert Indiana
American, born 1928

Costume design for Virgil T[homson]
in *The Mother of Us All*, 1976
Cut paper, 26 × 20 in.
Gift of Robert L. B. Tobin
1978.12.7

65

Robert Indiana
American, born 1928

Costume design for Lillian Russell
in *The Mother of Us All*, 1966
Cut paper, 26 × 19⅞ in.
Gift of Robert L. B. Tobin
1978.12.23

THE MAQUETTE AND CONTEMPORARY THEATRE

Maquettes, or scale models, are a favorite of visitors to the Tobin Collection. They make it possible to visualize how the designer's ideas translate from the drawing board to the three dimensions of the stage. In addition, maquettes, like annotated costume and scene renderings, invite viewers to participate in the process by which carpenters, painters, and costumers realize the designer's vision.

In the eighteenth and nineteenth centuries, drawings for, or prints of, painted drops and flats were cut out and assembled in a shadow box as they would appear on a proscenium stage. In the twentieth century, with the emergence of an architectural or sculptural as opposed to a painterly stage, maquettes have become essential to the building of sets, the blocking of movement, and the plotting of lighting.

Some designers are skilled creators of painter's elevations for the scene shop, gridded up for enlargement, or of construction diagrams for the costume shop, complete with fabric swatches. Others excel as maquette makers, resourcefully finding ways to convey their ideas in miniature. Today, many designers make use of computer assisted design (CAD) programs, but others believe that there is no replacement for the tactile beauty and technical utility of the maquette.

The aesthetics of maquettes vary widely, according to the demands of specific productions as well as the sensibilities of individual designers. From the minimal to the claustrophobic, the elegant to the ramshackle, the symbolic to the whimsical, all of the maquettes in the Tobin Collection are exciting and accessible examples of excellence in theatre design.

66
Jocelyn Herbert
British, 1917–2003

Maquette for *Lulu*, 1977
Painted wood, paper, and fabric,
23⅞ × 36¼ × 29¼ in.
Gift of the Tobin Endowment
TL2002.103.1
Opera by Alban Berg

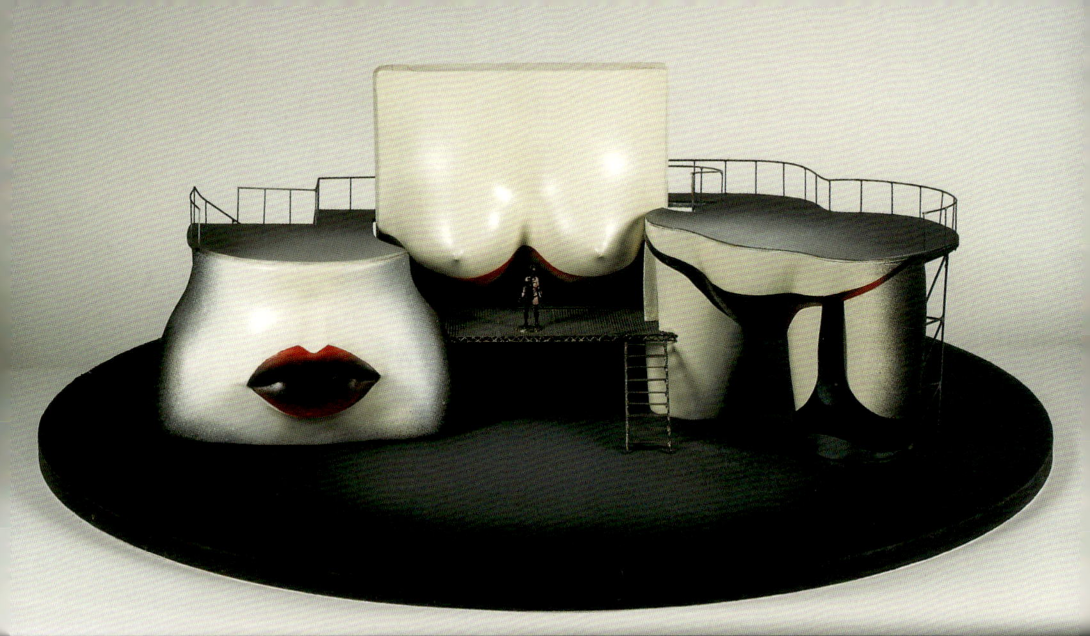

67
Ralph Koltai
British, born Germany, 1924

Maquette for *Die Soldaten (The Soldiers)*, 1983
Painted plastic with collage, metal, and found objects,
18 × 39 × 39 in.
Gift of the Tobin Endowment
TL2002.141
Opera by Bernd Alois Zimmermann

68
Tazeena Firth
British, born 1935

Timothy O'Brien
British, born 1929

Maquette for *The Bassarids*, 1974
Painted board with thread, glass beads, metal, and
found wood, 19½ × 28½ × 26½ in.
Gift of the Tobin Endowment
TL2002.192
Opera by Hans Werner Henze

69
Tony Straiges
American, born 1942

Maquette for Boys Bathing Unit in *Sunday in the
Park with George*, 1984
Painted paper and board with metal, 4½ × 9 × 5 in.
Gift of Robert L. B. Tobin
TL1999.321
Musical with lyrics and music by Stephen Sondheim

70
Marjorie Kellogg
American, born 1946

Maquette for Texas Flag Scrim in *The Best Little
Whorehouse in Texas*, 1978
Painted paper and fabric with thread and metal,
12½ × 18½ × 2 in.
Gift of Robert L. B. Tobin
TL1999.135
Musical with lyrics and music by Carol Hall

71
David Gallo
American, born 1966

Maquette for *You're a Good Man, Charlie Brown*, 1998
Painted and printed paper on board with papier-mâché,
21 × 31⅞ × 18 in.
Gift of the Tobin Foundation for Theatre Arts
TL2002.10
Musical with lyrics and music by Clark Gesner

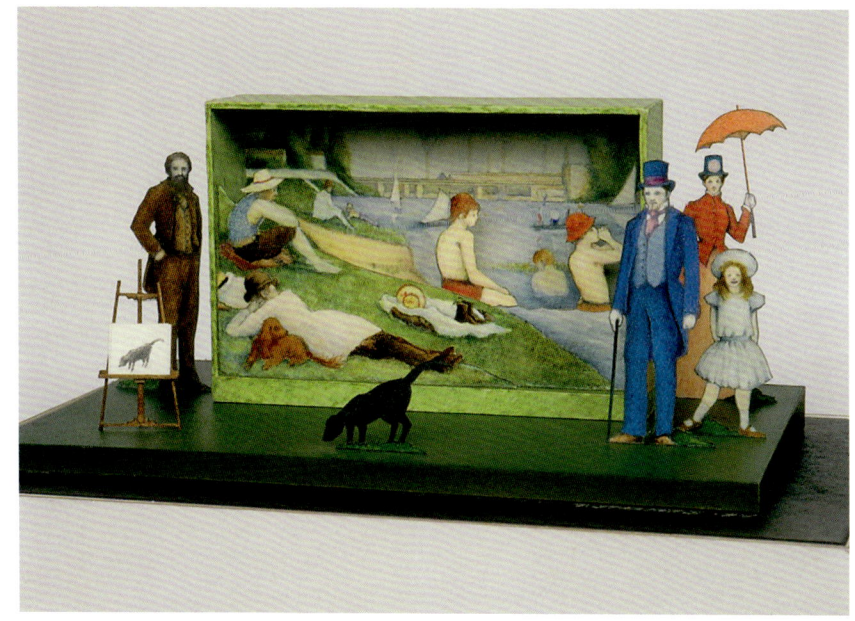

Jody Blake

ROBERT L. B. TOBIN AND THE THEATRE

Robert Lynn Batts Tobin (1934–2000) was a distinctive and commanding figure in San Antonio and in the international arts community. At nineteen, when his father was killed in an airplane crash, Robert Tobin took over the direction of Tobin Aerial Surveys, Inc. With his mother, Margaret Lynn Batts Tobin, he built it into an industry leader known for the graphic quality of its cartography. In addition to being a successful and prominent businessman, Tobin was a generous philanthropist and a visionary collector of theatre arts.

In South Texas, Batts and Tobin are legendary names. Robert Lynn Batts Tobin was proud of this heritage and cognizant of the responsibilities that came with it.

LEFT
Portrait by Karsh of Robert L. B. Tobin in his library at Oakwell Farms, ca. 1964.

NEAR RIGHT
Margaret Lynn Batts, ca. 1920.

FAR RIGHT
Edgar G. Tobin, ca. 1918.

LEFT
Margaret Lynn Batts Tobin with Robert, ca. 1937.

RIGHT
Edgar G. Tobin with Robert, ca. 1936.

Margaret Lynn Batts Tobin (1898–1989) was from a family of distinguished Texas jurists, including her father, Robert Lynn Batts, a University of Texas law professor and U.S. Circuit Court judge. Margaret Tobin, like her mother, Harriet Fiquet Batts, was a graduate of the University of Texas at Austin. Robert Tobin's father, Edgar Gardner Tobin (1897–1954), was a descendant of the founders of San Fernando de Bexar and of defenders of the Alamo. During the First World War, Edgar Tobin was a flying ace in the Lafayette Escadrille commanded by Eddie Rickenbacker.

Margaret and Edgar Tobin, like many philanthropic couples, embodied a potent combination of business acumen, cultivated taste, and a sense of civic responsibility, qualities they passed on to their son. Edgar Tobin capitalized on his flying skills by founding Tobin Aerial Surveys, Inc., an aerial mapping company serving the oil industry. Margaret Tobin was respected for her knowledge of art and music, creating her own important collection of modern art and serving on the boards of distinguished cultural institutions, including the McNay Art Museum; the San Antonio Symphony, which she helped found in 1939; and the Metropolitan Opera in New York.

Childhood photos of Robert Tobin underscore his precocious love of books, art, and music. He attended his first opera in Dallas at the tender age of six or seven—

ABOVE LEFT TO RIGHT

Robert L. B. Tobin with his grandmothers Ethel Tobin and Harriet Fiquet Batts and toys, including a toy grand piano, ca. 1937.

Robert L. B. Tobin with a book, ca. 1938.

Robert L. B. Tobin with paints, ca. 1942.

BELOW LEFT TO RIGHT

Robert L. B. Tobin (left) in San Antonio Opera Festival production of Modest Mussorgsky's *Boris Godunov*, 1959.

Robert L. B. Tobin (seated) as Sheridan Whiteside in Moss Hart and George S. Kaufman's *The Man Who Came to Dinner* at the San Antonio Little Theatre, ca. 1960.

Donizetti's *La Fille du Régiment* with soprano Lily Pons—and he was captivated. He responded by staging his own operas in a toy theatre, purchased from FAO Schwarz. By the time he was ten or twelve, Tobin had progressed to a dog kennel converted into a theatre on the grounds of his family's Terrell Hills estate.

During his years as a student in the Alamo Heights Independent School District, Tobin haunted Rosengren's bookstore, developing his taste for the rare and the beautiful. He reportedly requested artists' drawings and original theatre designs, rather than bikes or sports cars, as birthday and graduation gifts from his parents.

Tobin's formal education in theatre, at the University of Texas at Austin, was cut short when he took over the family business following his father's death in 1954. But his passion for the stage lasted a lifetime. As a young man, Tobin was active, both onstage and backstage, in the historic San Antonio Little Theatre (now the San Pedro Playhouse). He appeared in productions of the San Antonio Opera Festival,

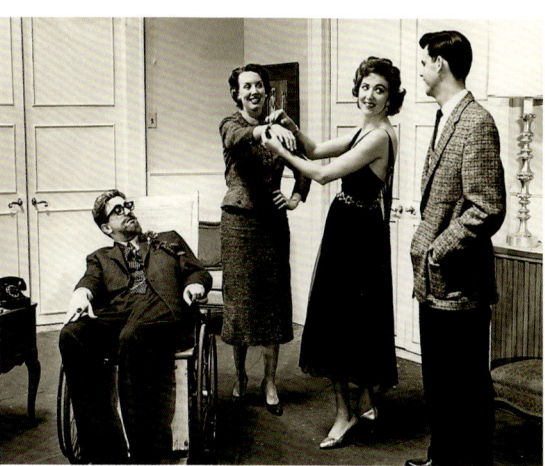

LEFT
First Lady Mrs. Lyndon B. Johnson escorted by Robert L. B. Tobin (right) and Marshall Steves at the performance of Verdi's *Don Carlos,* HemisFair, 1968.

RIGHT
Margaret Tobin and Robert L. B. Tobin attending an opening night performance at the Metropolitan Opera, ca. 1985.

established in 1945 by conductor Max Reiter, and served as its production coordinator from 1951 to 1963. He was also involved in design for and direction of this annual festival, culminating in a "surrealistic" production in 1970 of Mozart's *Don Giovanni,* starring Donald Gramm as Leporello.

When San Antonio hosted HemisFair in 1968, Margaret and Robert Tobin underwrote *Don Carlos* for the opening celebration. Honored guests included the First Lady, Mrs. Lyndon B. Johnson, who expressed her appreciation in an autographed photograph. The production featured designs by Yale University's Donald Oenslager that evoked Spanish cathedrals, gardens, and dungeons. This was the first time that the uncut version of Verdi's opera had been performed in the United States. The curtain rose in what is now the Lila Cockrell Theatre at 6 P.M., fell shortly before 1 A.M., and the evening was punctuated by a buffet dinner.

Journalists frequently used the expression "mother and son team" to describe the arts patronage of Margaret and Robert Tobin. Following in his mother's footsteps, Tobin served on the boards of numerous cultural institutions, including the McNay Art Museum, the San Antonio Symphony Society, the Museum of Modern Art in New York, the Metropolitan Opera, the Santa Fe Opera, the Opera Company of Boston, and the Festival of Two Worlds in Spoleto, Italy.

Robert L. B. Tobin (right) with Igor Stravinsky at the University of Texas at Austin, ca. 1965.

The Tobins helped underwrite numerous operas, including the United States premiere of Alban Berg's *Lulu* at the Santa Fe Opera Festival in 1963 and the original, uncut version of George Gershwin's *Porgy and Bess* at the Metropolitan Opera in 1985. As these productions suggest, the Tobins were known for their support of the twentieth-century repertoire, from Igor Stravinsky's *Rake's Progress* and Virgil Thomson's *The Mother of Us All* in Santa Fe to Benjamin Britten's *Peter Grimes* and Philip Glass's *The Voyage* at the Metropolitan. Designers whose work was supported by the Tobins included Eugene Berman, Jocelyn Herbert, Robert Indiana, and Timothy O'Brien. Their works are among the most important examples of contemporary scene and costume design in the Tobin Collection of Theatre Arts.

During his lifetime, Tobin exhibited his theatre collection in New York, Santa Fe, and Spoleto. In the end, however, San Antonio and the McNay Art Museum became the fortunate beneficiaries of the Tobins' passionate involvement with theatre arts in this country and abroad.

William J. Chiego

ROBERT L. B. TOBIN AND THE MCNAY

Robert Tobin was deeply involved with the McNay Art Museum from its inception. His mother, Margaret Lynn Batts Tobin, was among the museum's original trustees, and Robert became a friend to the McNay's first director, John Palmer Leeper, when he arrived in San Antonio in 1953. Although Tobin was barely twenty years old when the museum opened its doors to the public in 1954, he was already a serious art collector, having made his first acquisition, a Paul Klee watercolor, at the age of thirteen.

By 1956, the second full year of the museum's operation, Tobin was already a lender of works of art to the fledgling institution, beginning with a Eugene Berman exhibition that year. Shortly afterwards, Tobin was among the individuals invited by Leeper to form the McNay's first membership organization, created especially to support art acquisitions. He was active in the Friends of the McNay for many years, helping to select works for the annual Collectors Gallery and personally contributing funds for purchases through the Friends. In this way the museum received one of its first American painting acquisitions, a still life by Alfred Maurer.

In 1959, Tobin was instrumental in organizing an exhibition for the McNay of designs for the theatre by Norman Bel Geddes, Eugene Berman, and Marc Chagall to coincide with the meetings of the Southwest Theatre Conference in San Antonio. In this same year, he also lent the majority of works for the exhibition *Great Books and Great Editions.* And two years later, in 1961, he served on a panel discussing printmaking for *Printer's Ink,* an exhibition of important examples of modern graphic art borrowed from such great collections as the National Gallery of Art, the Art Institute of Chicago, and the Fogg Art Museum at Harvard University as well as from the private collection of Lessing J. Rosenwald.

This pattern of personal involvement and generous support would be repeated many times over the ensuing years, usually focusing on those areas of collecting that

Robert L. B. Tobin installing *Explosion: Color: Paris: 1909* at the McNay, 1969.

were most dear to Tobin's heart: theatre arts, the art of the book, prints and drawings, and American art. These interests remained strong throughout his life, and his generosity would result in the great enrichment of the McNay's collections in all of these areas.

There are several landmark events in Tobin's commitment to and involvement with the McNay. One of them was the 1969 exhibition *Explosion: Color: Paris: 1909*, which he organized for the museum from his own collection of designs from Diaghilev's Ballets Russes. This exhibition and its catalogue were featured at the 1970 Spoleto Festival of Two Worlds of which Tobin was the president. The exhibition demonstrates his early respect for and understanding of the Russian decorative tradition in stage design.

Showing the same keen perception he demonstrated in acquiring his Russian theatre designs, in 1972 he made another rare purchase at auction, Albert Gleizes's set of four paintings *Les Quatres Personnages Légendaires du Ciel (The Four Legendary Figures of the Sky)*, created for the Paris World's Fair of 1940. With his deep appreciation of the long history of fairs, festivals, and other forms of public theatre, Tobin recognized their importance and gave them to the McNay the following year.

At this time he also donated two notably rare works, Henri de Toulouse-Lautrec's 1893 lithograph of the dancer Loie Fuller, colored and dusted with gold by the artist himself, and George Grosz's painting of a different kind of performer, *Der Turner (The Gymnast)*, from the early 1920s. In these and other acquisitions, Tobin demonstrated

George Grosz
American, born Germany, 1893–1959

Der Turner (The Gymnast), ca. 1922
Oil on canvas, 41 × 31½ in.
Gift of Robert L. B. Tobin
1974.26

John Palmer Leeper (left), Robert L. B. Tobin, and Virgil Thomson (far right) at the exhibition of Robert Indiana's designs for *The Mother of Us All*, 1979.

a remarkable eye for strong design and the unusual, with a scholar's understanding of their significance.

In the field of theatre arts, among Tobin's greatest early gifts to the museum were the designs of his friend Robert Indiana for Virgil Thomson's opera *The Mother of Us All*, with libretto by Gertrude Stein. The opera was based on the life of Susan B. Anthony, the famous suffragette, and Indiana created brilliantly colorful Pop art designs for the Santa Fe Opera's 1976 production, which was sponsored by Tobin and his mother.

In the early 1970s, Tobin was invited to join the board of the Museum of Modern Art by its president, Mrs. John D. Rockefeller III; he accepted, but made it clear that his first allegiance would always be to the McNay as the future home of his collection, considering the museum a part of his family. Indeed, the following decade was punctuated by his continued generosity and personal interest in the growth of the McNay's collections and its exhibition program, culminating in a major gift and a long-term commitment from his mother and from Robert Tobin himself.

Eugene Berman
American, born Russia, 1899–1972

Portrait Fantasy of Ona Munson,
1941–42
Oil on canvas, 39½ × 28½ in.
Gift of Robert L. B. Tobin
1982.84

In the late 1970s and early 1980s, Tobin continued to underwrite exhibitions and to give handsomely to the print collection. One of the most important gifts was a complete first edition of Francisco de Goya's *The Disasters of War* (1810–14), the very first works by the great Spanish artist to enter the collection. But his gifts touched on many other high points of the graphic arts, including key works by Edouard Manet, Jacques Villon, Karl Schmidt-Rottluff, and David Hockney. Also during these years Tobin began to donate his great collection of works by his good friend Eugene Berman, the prolific Russian-born American artist who was both a painter and a leading designer for the theatre, most notably for the Metropolitan Opera in New York. Elected to the Metropolitan's governing board in 1975, Tobin was chairman of its centennial celebration in 1983. His devotion to the McNay was recognized by his election to the museum's board of trustees in 1981. At both the Metropolitan Opera and the McNay, Tobin served on the board alongside his mother.

In the early 1980s, Margaret Tobin, with the encouragement of McNay director John Palmer Leeper, began to give funds for the design of a library wing to house the remarkable theatre arts collection assembled over many years by her son, and also to provide badly needed space for the museum's rapidly growing art reference library. The plans for the new wing drew inspiration from Tobin's maternal grandfather's library as well as from his own library at his home in Oakwell, the family farm in San Antonio. Tobin began to donate his superb collection of rare books, primarily volumes from the seventeenth and eighteenth centuries, to be the cornerstone of the future Tobin Library. The building opened to the public on Robert Tobin's fiftieth birthday, March 12, 1984, and was dedicated by his mother to his grandparents, Robert Lynn Batts and Harriett Fiquet Batts.

Tobin's long personal involvement with the affairs of the McNay took on a new intensity with the opening of the Tobin Wing. Although his gifts to various areas of the collection continued, his primary focus turned to the exhibition program of theatre arts that the Tobin Library, expressly designed for this purpose, now made possible on a regular basis. The very first exhibition was *Eugene Berman and the Theatre of Melancholia* in 1984, which drew from Tobin's unparalleled collection of the artist's work. This groundbreaking exhibition, like Tobin's earlier show of designs for the Ballets Russes, was far ahead of its time. Thus began an uninterrupted parade of pioneering exhibitions from Tobin's vast collection of theatre arts, organized with

LEFT TO RIGHT

Robert L. B. Tobin speaking at the Gontcharova symposium, 1987.

Grand spiral staircase of the Tobin Wing under construction in 1984.

Linda Hardberger, who came to the McNay in 1984 as curator of the Tobin Collection of Theatre Arts. Over the following decade they collaborated on more than a dozen exhibitions, with Tobin writing introductory essays for each exhibition catalogue in his distinctive, exuberant prose style.

In addition to the exhibitions, in 1986 there began a series of seven major symposia on various eras of scene and costume design. All were sponsored by Tobin, usually in conjunction with an exhibition, and he often participated personally. The symposia were successful in bringing to San Antonio many of the leading designers for theatre as well as scholars of theatre arts, acquainting them with the riches of the Tobin Collection. Participants included designers Ming Cho Lee and Robin Wagner as well as scholars and curators Nancy Van Norman Baer, Mary Henderson, and John E. Bowlt.

Tobin was elected vice president of the McNay board of trustees in 1986, and elevated to chairman in 1990 after his mother's death the year before. During the late 1980s and early 1990s, Tobin continued to organize exhibitions and also assisted in many areas of the museum's operation, giving generously in his areas of greatest interest and supporting the further expansion of the museum's facilities. Major theatre arts gifts made during this time included more than seven hundred fifty drawings by Angelo and Camillo Parravicini for the opera, and a collection of more than five hundred books on the history of dance. With his encouragement, Tobin's mother also donated a rare collection of prints, drawings, and archival material by the legendary British designer Edward Gordon Craig. At this same time, Tobin augmented the museum's drawing collection with important works by Henry Moore, Robert Morris, and Cy Twombly, and ventured beyond his passion for works of art on paper to the sculpture collection, giving works by Alexandra Exter and Henry Moore and helping the museum to acquire works by Jean-Jacques Feuchère and Richard Stankiewicz.

Always a staunch supporter of improvements to the McNay's physical plant, Tobin provided a major gift to endow the Blanche and John Leeper Auditorium when the long-held dream of such a facility became a reality in 1994. The opening of the auditorium was followed almost immediately by celebrations of the tenth anniversary of the Tobin Wing. This was marked by the exhibition *Masterworks from the Tobin Collection of Theatre Arts,* the first comprehensive showing of the full range of the collection. In characteristic fashion, Tobin celebrated the occasion with additional gifts to the museum. He strengthened the American painting collection with major

George L. K. Morris
American, 1905–1975

Requiem for the Met, 1967
Oil on canvas, 45½ × 54¼ in.
Gift of Robert L. B. Tobin
1999.103

works by Marsden Hartley and Joan Mitchell, and the drawing collection with works by Charles Demuth, Andrew Wyeth, Paul Klee, and René Magritte. He also enhanced the theatre arts collection with a brilliant gift of seven models for Tim Burton's film *The Nightmare Before Christmas,* which Tobin acquired with the express purpose of providing youngsters a window into designing for the theatre.

By the mid-1990s, Tobin's health, fragile since surviving a major bout with cancer at the beginning of the decade, grew more precarious. His direct participation in organizing exhibitions lessened. However, there was no diminution in his passion for improving his collections or his generosity in sponsoring exhibitions in the Tobin Wing, including major traveling shows from other museums. Of equal importance was his endorsement of the museum's efforts to plan for the future; the Tobin Foundation supported a comprehensive study of the McNay's long-range space and site needs.

During his final years, Tobin accelerated the pace of his gifts to the McNay, beginning in 1998 with the donation of his great collection of Russian scene and costume designs, primarily in the decorative style. This body of work included more than six hundred objects, with especially notable designs by Natalia Gontcharova, Mikhail Larionov, Léon Bakst, and Alexandre Benois. The following year Tobin gave his important collection of more than one thousand American scene and costume designs, and, as a parallel gift, he invited the McNay's director to choose works for the museum from his varied collection of American paintings. Capping his many gifts to the American collection over the years, this new selection included rare modernist works by William Zorach, James Daugherty, George L. K. Morris, and Paul Cadmus, as well as postwar works by Joan Mitchell and Robert Indiana that strengthened his earlier gift of works by these two artists.

Tobin recognized the critical need to renovate the McNay's environmental systems and to restore the 1920s home of Marion Koogler McNay, which is the museum's historical core. He pledged a lead gift of two million dollars to help fund these much-needed improvements, intended to ensure the proper care of the collection.

When Robert L. B. Tobin died in April 2000, he had made arrangements to complete the gift of his entire theatre arts collection. Thus, in the succeeding years the museum received a major group of works by twentieth-century artists whose reputations as painters or sculptors equaled or exceeded their renown as designers for the theatre. Included were designs by Pablo Picasso, Henri Matisse, Eugene Berman, Louise Nevelson, and David Hockney. The most recent gift was Tobin's rich collection of twentieth-century European work, primarily contemporary British designs that reflect his strong interest in experimental productions. Included were designs by Edward Gordon Craig, Oliver Messel, Tanya Moiseiwitsch, Cecil Beaton, Ralph Koltai, and Timothy O'Brien.

Thanks to continued support by the Tobin Foundation for Theatre Arts, funded by the Tobin Endowment, for exhibitions, acquisitions, and internships in theatre arts, the programs initiated by Tobin have continued at the McNay, fulfilling his desire to make this great collection as accessible as possible to the theatre community and to the general public. With the help of the Tobin Endowment, the McNay has been able to maintain a strong curatorial vision for the collection. The final gift planned by Tobin, to be made in the near future, will further cement the McNay's status as the leading center in the United States for the exhibition and study of the theatre arts. For that we can be grateful for the collecting passion, the intellectual curiosity, and the remarkable generosity of Robert L. B. Tobin.

TRIBUTES TO ROBERT L. B. TOBIN

Robert Tobin received numerous honors for his contributions to the arts. The recognition that meant the most to him, however, came from people who worked in the theatre. In 1994 the Association of Design, Production, and Technology Professionals in the Performing Arts presented him with the USITT Award for lifetime achievement. This award from the United States Institute for Theatre Technology put Tobin in the company of many of the designers he admired and whose work he collected. The respect that Tobin gained from theatre designers and historians is reflected in the remembrances below.

It is not only the quantity of Robert Tobin's collection, spanning more than three centuries, but also the great diversity of style and wit revealed about its collector that make it so wonderful and breathtaking. Robert liked notoriety, strength, and brashness in the work. He cared little about the public opinion of the piece.... His tastes were eclectic and brave. He liked nothing more than to reintroduce an audience to a particular work. Because he was not the artist of the work, he perhaps loved and possessed it more than its creator. This was his passion.

—Robert Perdziola, theatre designer, New York; recipient of the Irene Sharaff Young Master Award for costume design and the Helen Hayes Award for costume design

Robert Perdziola
American, born 1961

Scene design for *Ariadne auf Naxos*, ca. 1997–98
Watercolor and graphite on paper,
8⅜ × 12⅝ in.
Gift of Robert L. B. Tobin
TL1999.236.19
Opera by Richard Strauss

∼

Robert Tobin was the ringmaster of a traveling circus of faith in the theatrical form. This he never abandoned. Using his wealth of energy and unlimited enthusiasm, he kept the intentions and memories of very many designers alive by standing between the studio and the dustcart; and awakening designers to the value of their work. If he arrived at your door to see what he could add to his Gontcharova, Bakst, Messel, and Berman, he did wonders for your morale, and took your eye off the dustbin. He has done theatre history a great service.

—Timothy O'Brien, theatre designer, London; fellow of the Royal Society of Arts, recipient of the Gold Medal for set design and the Golden Triga for best national exhibit at the Prague Quadrennial

∼

There are people who are only interested in the objects. They are not interested in the people who created those objects. Robert was the absolute opposite. He was a friend of all the people who create. His taste was broad, eclectic, and he made very few value judgments based on trends. So his collection embodies a great range of work. Robert was a person who treated the work—the visual part of the performing arts, theatre, opera—as a living force, not as dead objects. And [his collection] continues to support it, to speak for it, and to bring young people into the arts.

—Ming Cho Lee, professor of Design and chair of the Design Department at the Yale School of Drama; recipient of the Tony Award for scene design, the USITT Award for lifetime achievement, and the National Medal of Arts

∼

The thing I loved most about Robert Tobin was his love of the artist who made theatre happen.... I find it very flattering to be a designer collected by Tobin. It's a seal of approval.... Tobin's legacy is very much alive in the fact that the Tobin Collection is beautifully looked after, the fact that it spreads its wings, it helps students, it helps professionals, it helps everyone. And to me that's a living thing. Robert's legacy is one of great joy.

—Desmond Heeley, theatre designer, New York; recipient of Tony Awards for scene and costume design and the Irene Sharaff Lifetime Achievement Award for costume design

Desmond Heeley
British, born 1931

Costume design for Heralds, Act I, Scene 3 in *Henry IV*, 1964
Watercolor, graphite and metallic paint, 9¹¹⁄₁₆ × 7⅜ in.
Gift of the Tobin Endowment, TL2002.95.1
Play by William Shakespeare

≈

The great American scenic designer Lee Simonson once wrote: "A scenic drawing is no more than a record of intention, without value except as it is realized in the theatre." Robert L. B. Tobin thought otherwise. The tangible design on paper is often the only evidence that a play was performed within the scenic environment depicted on the very paper that survived the production. Somehow, the soul of the play resides in the design and, perhaps, this was the reason that led Tobin to amass the thousands of scene renderings that formed his unique collection. Another reason is suspected. Unlike Simonson, Tobin considered them works of fine art deserving to be preserved and exhibited in a museum, not merely records of intention.

—Mary C. Henderson, curator emerita, Theatre Collection of the Museum of the City of New York

≈

To Robert Tobin the performing arts both delighted the senses and engaged the intellect; in their manifold manifestations (opera, ballet, drama, cabaret) and attributes (costumes, backdrops, props) they inspired passionate license and aesthetic debate, qualities that guided his acquisitions and molded the composition of his magnificent collection, now at the McNay Museum.

Although the assemblage is vast and diverse, one of the primary strengths is the Russian representation. Robert regarded the Russian stage, especially the Ballets Russes, as the greatest monument to the Silver Age of Russian culture. Indeed, there was something in his physical stature and captivating eye that allied him with other celebrated impresarios of Russian arts and letters, not least Sergei Diaghilev.

—John E. Bowlt, professor of Slavic Languages and Literatures, University of Southern California, Los Angeles

Linda Hardberger

A PERSONAL REMEMBRANCE

When I went to my interview with John Leeper, director of the McNay Art Museum at the time, for the position of curator of the Tobin Collection, I discovered that Robert Tobin also was participating in the interview. Little did I realize then the influence that he would have on my professional and personal life for the next sixteen years. What a true adventure those years were, and, I expect, will continue to be.

Workers were putting the finishing touches on the new Tobin wing on January 2, 1984, my first working day at the McNay. When I arrived that morning, I was confronted with numerous crates spread throughout the Brown Gallery waiting to be opened, catalogued, and put on the shelves of the new library. Knowing, I am sure, that I would be overwhelmed by this scene, Tobin was there every day as we unpacked crates and put his outstanding collection of rare books on the shelves. Each object had a tale to tell, and he was the willing storyteller and I the willing listener. This close collaboration lasted until his death. Throughout those years Tobin continued to be my compass, gently guiding me from one discovery to the next. No explorer ever had a better or more enthusiastic guide.

Tobin never directed or corrected—he quietly suggested. As a teacher, he believed in self-discovery. I was never told how to mount an exhibition; it was assumed I would know how. His guidance was subtle but informed, his memory truly amazing. He knew every piece in his collection and where it was. He knew the contents of every festival book—those books published after each royal festival in Europe from the sixteenth through the nineteenth centuries—regardless of the language, even though he only spoke English. Because he was interested not only in the object but also in its creator, many of the designers included in the collection became personal friends of his.

Tobin was a man who could best be described as an imposing figure without being daunting, comfortable rather than stuffy, and a singular storyteller who often began his sentences with, "Did I ever tell you…?" He was also an avid sports fan and an animal lover. He was equally at home on a ranch, in museum storage rooms, at

Robert L. B. Tobin, Phillip Hardberger, and Linda Hardberger at the opening of *Paperworks* at the McNay Art Museum, 1985.

Metropolitan Opera openings, or looking out over the hills of Santa Fe. He could easily be discussing the merits of a designer's style one moment and in the next ask about one's pet or child, or critique last weekend's Cowboys game.

But theatre and art were Robert Tobin's life. A life that he willingly shared with anyone who took the time to look and/or listen. Generous to a fault, Tobin continued the family legacy of leadership and vision in the arts, devoting his energy and resources to the international arts community. His gifts to the Tobin Collection of Theatre Arts over the last twenty years have made the McNay Art Museum a leader in the United States for the exhibition and study of scene and costume design—a major accomplishment in and of itself. But what he really hoped was that by being exposed to this wonderfully eclectic collection we would discover that the history of theatre is not a chronologically ordered collection of images, but a visual record of moments in time when artists, using every trick they could conjure, overwhelmed reality with magic. All those who venture into the McNay, myself included, are and will continue to be the beneficiaries of his wish. I am honored to have known and worked with Robert L. B. Tobin, and I hope to do my small part in continuing his legacy.

TOBIN COLLECTION PUBLICATIONS

Listed below are catalogues for exhibitions organized by the Tobin Collection of Theatre Arts at the McNay Art Museum:

Eugene Berman and the Theatre of Melancholia, 1984. Organized by Linda Hardberger. Essay by Robert L. B. Tobin.

From Word to Image, 1984. Organized by Linda Hardberger. Essay by Robert L. B. Tobin.

Bakst and Benois, 1985. Organized by Linda Hardberger. Essay by Robert L. B. Tobin.

Paperworks, 1985. Organized by Linda Hardberger. Essay by Robert L. B. Tobin.

The Operatic Muse: An Exhibition of Works from the Robert L. B. Tobin Collection Honoring the 30th Anniversary Season of the Santa Fe Opera, 1986. Organized by Linda Hardberger. Essay by Robert L. B. Tobin.

Perspective Perceived, 1986. Organized by Linda Hardberger. Essay by Robert L. B. Tobin.

Robert Edmond Jones and the American Theatre, 1986. Organized by Linda Hardberger. Essay by Robert L. B. Tobin.

Gontcharova/Larionov, 1987. Organized by Linda Hardberger. Essay by Robert L. B. Tobin.

Paperworks II, 1987. Organized by Linda Hardberger. Essay by Robert L. B. Tobin.

Thespis Adorned, 1987. Organized by Linda Hardberger. Essay by Robert L. B. Tobin.

Courtly Splendor, 1988. Organized by Linda Hardberger. Essay by Robert L. B. Tobin.

Balletomania, 1990. Organized by Linda Hardberger. Essay by Robert L. B. Tobin.

The Broadway Scene, 1990. Organized by Linda Hardberger. Essay by Robert L. B. Tobin.

Procession, 1991. Organized by Linda Hardberger. Essay by Robert L. B. Tobin.

Entirely Mozart, 1992. Organized by Linda Hardberger. Essay by Robert L. B. Tobin.

Six Operas: Six Artists, 1992. Organized by Linda Hardberger. Essay by Robert L. B. Tobin.

Arch Lauterer, Henry J. Kurth, and John R. Rothgeb: A Teacher and His Student, 1993. Organized by Linda Hardberger. Essay by Henry J. Kurth.

Twentieth-Century British Stage Design, 1993. Organized by Linda Hardberger. Essay by Robert L. B. Tobin.

Masterworks from the Tobin Collection of Theatre Arts, 1994. Organized by Linda Hardberger. Essay by Linda Hardberger.

The New Stagecraft: Setting an American Style, 1915–1949, 1997. Organized by Linda Hardberger. Essay by Linda Hardberger.

The Garden Setting: Nature Designed, 1998. Organized by Linda Hardberger. Essay by Linda Hardberger.

Out of Russia: A Gift of Scene Design from Robert L. B. Tobin, 1999. Organized by Linda Hardberger. Essay by Linda Hardberger.

Setting the Stage American Style: A Gift of Scene Design from Robert L. B. Tobin, 2000. Organized by Linda Hardberger. Essay by Mary C. Henderson.

From Studios to Stages: A Promised Gift of Theatre Designs from the Robert L. B. Tobin Estate, 2001. Organized by Linda Hardberger. Essay by Linda Hardberger.

Mostly British: Scene and Costume Design of the 20th Century, 2002. Organized by Jody Blake. Essay by Arnold Wengrow.